PERCEPTION AND
THE PHYSICAL WORLD

International Library of Philosophy and Scientific Method

EDITOR: TED HONDERICH

A Catalogue of books already published in the
International Library of Philosophy and Scientific Method
will be found at the end of this volume.

PERCEPTION AND THE PHYSICAL WORLD

by

David Malet

D. M. Armstrong

B.A., Ph.D., Lecturer in Philosophy
University of Melbourne

LONDON

ROUTLEDGE & KEGAN PAUL

NEW YORK : THE HUMANITIES PRESS

First published *1961*
by Routledge & Kegan Paul Ltd.
Broadway House, 68-74 Carter Lane
London, E.C.4
Reprinted 1963, 1966, 1970

Printed in Great Britain by
Compton Printing Ltd.
London & Aylesbury.

ISBN 0 7100 3603 5

CONTENTS

ACKNOWLEDGEMENTS   *page* ix

INTRODUCTION   xi

PART ONE: ARE THE SENSIBLE QUALITIES SUBJECTIVE?

1   ARGUMENTS TO PROVE THE SENSIBLE QUALITIES SUB-
JECTIVE   3
(1) The Argument from Sensation   3
(2) The Argument from the Relativity of sensible qualities   10
(3) The Argument from Illusion   14

PART TWO: THE ARGUMENT FROM ILLUSION

2   WHAT ARE THE IMMEDIATE OBJECTS OF AWARENESS IN
PERCEPTION?   19

3   REFUTATION OF THE REPRESENTATIVE THEORY OF
PERCEPTION   28
(1) We have no reason to believe in the existence of the
physical objects postulated by the Representative
theory   29
(2) On the Representative theory, there can be no resemblance between sense-impressions and physical objects   31
(3) The conception of a physical object which cannot be
immediately perceived is illogical   33

4   SOME FEATURES OF SENSE-IMPRESSIONS   35
(1) Can there be sense-impressions nobody has?   35
(2) Are sense-impressions just as they appear to be?   37

5   REFUTATION OF PHENOMENALISM (1)   47
(1) The Phenomenalist gives unperceived physical objects
a merely hypothetical existence   53
(2) The Phenomenalist must admit that a universe that contains no minds contains no matter either   56
(3) Physical objects, which are determinate, cannot be constructions out of indeterminate sense-impressions   58

CONTENTS

6 REFUTATION OF PHENOMENALISM (2) *page* 62
  (4) Difficulties for the Phenomenalist account of Space and
    Time 62
  (5) Phenomenalism can give no account of the numerical
    difference of minds that exist at the same time 67
  (6) Phenomenalism can give no satisfactory account of the
    nature of a mind 70

7 AN ANALYSIS OF SENSORY ILLUSION 80
  (1) Sensory illusion as false belief that we are perceiving 81
  (2) 'Perception without belief' 84
  (3) Is 'perception without belief' *essentially* belief-inducing? 87
  (4) A psychological explanation of the occurrence of some
    sensory illusions 93

PART THREE: THE ARGUMENT FROM
VERIFICATION

8 THE ARGUMENT FROM VERIFICATION 101

9 THE NATURE OF PERCEPTION 105
  (1) Perception always involves the acquiring of knowledge
    of particular facts about the physical world, by means
    of our senses 107
  (2) Perception is *nothing but* the acquiring of knowledge of
    particular facts about the physical world by means of
    our senses 112

10 CONSEQUENCES OF OUR ACCOUNT OF THE NATURE OF
  PERCEPTION 123
  (1) The existence of unconscious perception 123
  (2) Are there intermediate cases between veridical and
    illusory perception? 124
  (3) Reformulation of the Empiricist theory of the way we
    acquire empirical concepts 125
  (4) The distinction between sensory illusion and hallucina-
    tion 126
  (5) The Nature of sense-impressions 127
  (6) The Argument from Verification answered 132

PART FOUR: THE ARGUMENT FROM CAUSATION

11 THE ARGUMENT FROM CAUSATION 139
  (1) The Argument from Causation 141
  (2) The Argument from the Time-gap 144

CONTENTS

PART FIVE: THE ARGUMENT FROM SCIENCE

12   THE ARGUMENT FROM SCIENCE   *page* 155
     (1) Scientific Phenomenalism   156
     (2) Difficulties for Scientific Phenomenalism   158

13   DIRECT REALISM WITHOUT SCIENTIFIC PHENOMENALISM   165
     (1) Can scientific findings undermine perception?   166
     (2) The argument from paradigm cases   167

14   PROBLEMS ABOUT THE SECONDARY QUALITIES   172
     (1) The apparent simplicity of the secondary qualities   172
     (2) Are the secondary qualities really simple?   174
     (3) Can the secondary qualities be reduced to primary
         qualities?   176

15   CAN PHYSICAL OBJECTS HAVE NOTHING BUT THE PRIMARY
     QUALITIES?   184

     CONCLUSION   191

     INDEX   194

ACKNOWLEDGEMENTS

THE following persons have read and commented on various drafts of this book: Professor D. A. T. Gasking, Dr. A. C. Jackson, both of the University of Melbourne, Mr. D. C. Stove of the University of Sydney, and Professor J. J. C. Smart of the University of Adelaide. They have saved me from much error and obscurity, and have made many positive suggestions. I am profoundly grateful to them.

I have had a number of very helpful conversations with Dr. C. B. Martin of the University of Adelaide. Professor H. H. Price, who was once my supervisor in Oxford, has read and commented on, with characteristic patience and ingenuity, a number of my earlier pieces on the philosophy of perception. What he has said has helped me very much in writing the present work.

I originally learnt to accept the Direct Realist theory of perception, which is defended in this book, as an undergraduate in Sydney under Professor John Anderson. Those who know his work will perceive the extent of his influence on mine, perhaps even where I am unaware of it. There is much in this essay which he would not accept, but there is also much in it that I have learnt from him.

D. M. A.

University of Melbourne,
June 1960

INTRODUCTION

THERE is a triad of 'theories of perception' which compete for the allegiance of philosophers: Direct Realism, Representationalism and Phenomenalism. Each may be conceived of as an answer to the question 'What is the *direct* or *immediate* object of awareness when we perceive?' Direct Realism answers that the immediate object of awareness is never anything but a physical existent, which exists independently of the awareness of it. In opposition to this, Representationalism and Phenomenalism hold that the immediate object of awareness is a *sense-impression* or *sense-datum*, and such an object, it is usually assumed, cannot exist independently of the awareness of it. But Representationalism and Phenomenalism themselves divide over the question 'What is a physical object?' The Representationalist holds that physical objects are not to be identified with the immediate objects of awareness, but are quite distinct from, and capable of existing independently of, these immediate objects. The Phenomenalist, on the other hand, holds that physical objects are nothing more than constructions out of the immediate objects of awareness, and so holds that physical objects do not exist independently of perception.

These theories may be held in many different forms, and in some cases the lines of distinction may be blurred. But, for good or for ill, this question 'What is the direct or immediate object of awareness when we perceive?' has been the main question asked about perception in modern Western philosophy, and the answers to the question have taken one of these three general forms.

This means that any large-scale philosophical discussion of perception has an obligation to discuss this question. We must either accept one of the traditional answers, propose a new one, or else give reasons for thinking that the question itself is meaningless or confused, and so to be dissolved.

However, some modern philosophers seem to assume that the issue between Direct Realism, on the one hand, and Representationalism and Phenomenalism, on the other, is simply the question

'Do we perceive physical objects or not?' 'Do we ever see trees, touch stones, or hear trains?' The only answer can be that of course we do, and so Direct Realism has been taken as true but perfectly trivial, while its opponents have been taken to be saying something so absurd that only a philosopher would be capable of taking it seriously. And it must be admitted that some Representationalists and Phenomenalists have been so naïve as to assert that we do not perceive physical objects, while some Direct Realists have been deceived by these assertions into thinking that they are simply defending the triviality that we *do* perceive physical objects. But the real question at issue is 'What is the *direct* or *immediate* object of awareness when we perceive?'

It might be said that the meaning of the words 'direct' and 'immediate' is quite obscure, and that until they have been *given* some meaning, if they can be given any, this question about the direct or immediate object of awareness is no question at all. But I hope to show that the question is a perfectly precise and definite one, and that it is not to be answered off-hand, in the off-hand way that we can say that the things we perceive are physical objects. It is true that this is not a scientific question, to be answered by observation and experiment, but is a conceptual question, to be answered by the means appropriate to the discussion of a conceptual question, viz. philosophical argument. But it is just as real a question as, say, the conceptual question 'What is an unconscious wish?'

I hold that the Direct Realist answer to the question 'What is the *direct* or *immediate* object of awareness when we perceive?' is the correct one, and this book is a defence of Direct Realism. I shall discuss in turn what I take to be the main lines of objection to Direct Realism, try to answer them, and at the same time present what I take to be decisive objections to Representationalism and Phenomenalism. But in the course of the book I hope also to ask and answer the questions 'What is perception?', 'What is a sense-impression?', and even to cast some indirect light on the question 'What is a physical object?'.

If the reader wishes to get to the positive doctrines of this book as soon as possible, he can omit chapter 3, concerned with the refutation of the Representative theory of perception, and the two chapters (5 and 6), concerned with the refutation of Phenomenalism.

PART ONE

Are the Sensible Qualities Subjective?

ARGUMENTS TO PROVE THE SENSIBLE QUALITIES SUBJECTIVE

IN this chapter I will examine three arguments which purport to prove that some or all of the sensible qualities of objects have no existence except for a perceiving subject. By 'sensible qualities' are meant such qualities as colour, shape, size, motion, hardness, heat, sound, taste and smell, qualities of objects which are said to be perceived by the senses. These three arguments are all to be found in Berkeley's 'First Dialogue'. We shall see that each of these arguments is invalid. But each of them raises interesting points, and the third argument, although clearly invalid as it stands, is capable of being reformulated as an argument for a certain answer to the question 'What is the direct or immediate object of awareness when we perceive?'

I. THE ARGUMENT FROM SENSATION[1]

The object of the Argument from Sensation is to show that the sensible qualities of objects are nothing but species of *sensations*. Berkeley takes *physical pain* as a paradigm case of a sensation. Now sensations are mind-dependent, or subjective. A sensation demands the existence of a person conscious of having it, somebody

[1] Cf. The Works of George Berkeley Vol. 2. edited T. E. Jessop, pp. 175–181.

who feels it. So if the sensible qualities of things could be shown to be on all fours with what are ordinarily called sensations, it would follow that the sensible qualities would have been shown to be mind-dependent, or subjective.

In fact, however, Berkeley's argument is not very convincing. He takes the sensible quality of *heat*, which is one of the cases where the assimilation of sensible qualities to sensations is most plausible. He argues that if we treat any particular degree of heat as a sensation then we must treat all degrees of heat as sensations. But, he goes on, it cannot be denied that a very great heat is a great pain. Hence it is a sensation. It follows that any degree of heat is a sensation.

Berkeley considers the objection that great heat is not identical with great pain, but is only the *cause* of the pain. But he replies to this by saying that when, for instance, our hand is too near the fire, we only 'perceive one simple uniform sensation'. There is no possibility of distinguishing heat and pain.

But to see that Berkeley is wrong here, we do not have to investigate the unclear and difficult question whether our sensation is really simple and uniform in such a case. A very simple argument suffices to show that heat must be different from pain. For at different times our tolerance of heat can be quite different. What was once a painful heat, may become a *painful* heat no longer. Now if the very same heat is sometimes painful, but is sometimes not painful, this shows that there is some distinction to be made between heat and pain.

Now Berkeley would certainly reply to this argument by saying that, where I acquire a greater tolerance of heat, we have a case where the object in question *does not feel so hot*. And it is true, of course, that we do talk in this way. As we settle into a bath we say that the hot water gradually feels less hot, even where the actual temperature of the water is not falling. But this reply is really nothing to Berkeley's purpose. What he is trying to prove is that heat, a quality of physical objects, is a sensation. It will do him no good to prove that the pain varies in exact proportion to the heat that an object *feels to have to a person at a particular time*. For when we talk of the heat that an object feels to have to a person at a particular time we are not talking about the quality of an object; but about the person's impression of the heat of the object. We distinguish between an object having a certain colour, and its looking

4

to somebody to have a certain colour. In the same way we distinguish between an object being hot, and its feeling hot to us. Putting the matter more controversially, but conveniently, we distinguish between the qualities of objects, and our sense-impressions of these qualities. So to argue that, when the touching of a hot object causes us less pain, then the object does not feel so hot to us, would prove at best that our *sense-impressions* of heat are simply sensations. It would do nothing to show that any quality of a physical object, such as the quality heat, is a sensation. It is true, of course, that Berkeley fails to make a distinction between sensible qualities and sense-impressions, passing between the two with an ease born of oversight. But there *is* a distinction between a thing's actual heat, and the heat it feels to us to have on a particular occasion. If Berkeley wishes to deny the existence of such a distinction he is simply wrong. (What *account* we give of the distinction may be another matter.)

But not only is it incorrect to identify heat and pain, it is completely mistaken to treat any sensible quality as any sort of sensation. For there are a number of things that it makes sense to say of sensations, but not of sensible qualities, and vice-versa.

(i) In the first place, we say that we see the colours, shapes, sizes, motions and spatial relations of things, we say we taste the tastes of things, smell the smell of things, hear the sounds things emit, touch hot things and so on. To use a more general term, we say that we *perceive* the sensible qualities of things. But we do not say that we perceive sensations, rather we say that we *have* them, or that we *feel* them. If I have a pain in my leg I do not say that I perceive that there is a pain there, I say I have it or feel it. Berkeley is very misleading here because in the course of his argument on heat, and elsewhere, he says that pains do not exist unperceived. This implies that pains do exist when perceived. But in fact it is wrong to say that pains can either be perceived or not perceived. What Berkeley should have said, of course, is that pains and other sensations cannot exist *unhad* or *unfelt*. There cannot be a pain or a tickle which nobody has got, or which nobody is feeling. The 'esse' of sensations is not 'percipi' but 'sentiri'. But Berkeley, because he wants to *assimilate* the sensible qualities of things to sensations, wrongly says that sensations cannot exist unperceived.

This point may be dismissed as a *mere* point of language, or

B   5

nuance of linguistic convention. And in any case there is one piece of linguistic evidence which we have ignored, and which tells in Berkeley's favour. In the case of perception *by touch*, we do use the word 'feel'. We feel the pain, but we also feel the heat of the fire, the roughness of the material or the stickiness of the glue. (That is why Berkeley's assimilation of *heat* to a sensation has rather more plausibility than the assimilation of some other sensible qualities of objects.) And so Berkeley might defend himself by saying that, although by linguistic accident it is improper to say that a pain is perceived, it is proper to say that a pain is felt. Then he might argue that the example of feeling heat shows that feeling is a species of perception. For this reason, our use of the word 'perceive' in the case of the sensible qualities does not, by itself, suffice to show that Berkeley is wrong in assimilating the two classes of things to each other.

(ii) But we can produce a much more decisive point of differentiation. Perception of the sensible qualities of things always implies the possibility of misperception. But it is not possible to be wrong about the sensations we are having in the same sort of way. I may say that I perceive that an object is coloured grey. But it always makes sense to say that the object is not really grey, but only seems grey to me. Again I may say that I feel the great heat of the water, or the high temperature of my body. But it always makes sense to say that the water is not hot, or that I have not got a temperature, and that it only seems to me that the water is hot, or my body-temperature high. But suppose I say I feel pain. It does not make sense to say that I only seem to be feeling pain. There is no distinction to be made between getting it wrong and getting it right. It is possible for me to be mistaken about the *causes* of my pain; for instance, I might assign a certain physical cause to it when the pain was really psychological in origin. My sensation might be so slight that I might hesitate whether I was right to describe it as 'pain'. But although I may be mistaken about the causes of my sensations, or hesitate about their exact description, I cannot be mistaken about feeling them. But what I take to be my perceptions of sensible qualities can be mistaken.

At this point we are called on to consider the traditional example of the man who has lost a leg, but still feels pain in the place where the amputated leg was. Is he not mistaken in his sensations? The first point to be made is that he cannot be mistaken about thinking he has a pain, the very most he can be said to be mistaken about is the *location* of the pain. So pain still remains in a different category from colour, heat, taste, etc.

Can he even be mistaken about the location of the pain? If the location of the pain means the place of the *cause* of the pain, then clearly he can be mistaken. But does it mean this? If a man says he has a pain where his amputated limb used to be, are we prepared to say that he does not really have the pain there? If somebody thinks he has a pain in a certain place, that is where he has the pain; and if he says he feels it to be where his leg used to be, then that is the place where the pain is. A pain is where it feels to be. So nothing at all in this case need shake our sharp distinction between sensations and the sensible qualities of objects.

The fact that we can be wrong about the sensible qualities of objects, but cannot be wrong about our sensations, gives us a useful test in cases where it is disputed whether we are dealing with an actual property of objects or a mere bodily sensation. Suppose somebody asserts that tastes are simply sensations, for instance. This seems to be wrong, because we do distinguish between a thing tasting bitter to me on a certain occasion, and its really being bitter. This is clearly marked off from e.g. the tingling of the tongue that a certain substance may cause, because we do not distinguish between an apparent tingle and a real one.

(iii) In the third place, the sensible qualities of physical objects can be perceived by anybody who is suitably placed, and whose sense-organs are in a suitable condition. But only I can feel my sensations.

(iv) Finally, it may be pointed out, the qualities of physical objects can still qualify the objects even when nobody is perceiving them. The water is hot, the wall is white, although there is nobody to feel the water or see the wall. But a sensation cannot exist unfelt. We may 'scarcely feel' our pains, or pay little attention to them if they are mild, but we cannot dispense with feeling them altogether. If we do not feel the pain at all, we are not *in pain*. The same seems to be true of all sensations.

For all these reasons, then, it seems clear that sensible qualities of things cannot be sensations.

But the collapse of the Argument from Sensation leads on to a further question of interest and importance. Granted that Berkeley

7

was quite wrong to treat sensible qualities as sensations, is it not correct to identify *sense-impressions* with sensations? When an object looks to me to be blue, when, as a psychologist would say, there is something blue in my visual field, is this not like having a pain or feeling a tickle, and so equally to be called a *sensation*? Berkeley regularly talks about 'ideas or sensations', sense-impressions being the most important class of things covered by his word 'idea'. Berkeley, as we have seen, fails to make any clear distinction between the sensible qualities of things and our sense-impressions of these qualities. But we can make the distinction, and then suggest that, although it may be wrong to identify the sensible qualities with sensations, it would be perfectly right to treat sense-impressions as sensations.

In support of this suggestion it can be pointed out that if we use the tests that established a clear distinction between the sensible qualities of things and sensations we shall find that, in each case, sense-impressions resemble sensations. (i) We do not naturally say that we *perceive* our sense-impressions, rather we say that we *have* them, just as we say that we *have* certain sensations. (ii) In the same way that we cannot be mistaken about our sensations we cannot be mistaken about our sense-impressions either. It is very odd to say 'I think I am in pain'. The question of being wrong does not come up, or at any rate it does not come up in the clear and obvious way that it comes up for the perception of the sensible qualities of things. (iii) Again, only I can have my sense-impressions, just as only I can have my sensations. (iv) Finally, just as sensations cannot exist unhad, so sense-impressions cannot exist unhad either. A sense-impression implies the existence of somebody to have it.[1]

Moved by these extensive resemblances, many thinkers have failed to make any distinction between sensations and sense-impressions. We find many philosophers and psychologists who are prepared to talk indifferently of a sensation of pain, a sensation of heat, a sensation of blue and a sensation of extension.

This idiom seems rather unnatural in the case of colours, and even more so in the case of extension, but in the case of heat, for example, 'sensation' and 'sense-impression' do seem to be interchangeable terms. When my hand feels hot, we could speak in-

[1] We shall, however, reconsider these points about sense-impressions in chap. 4.

differently of sensations of heat in my hand or sense-impressions of heat in my hand.

Nevertheless, there are some sensations—pains are one case—which are different from sense-impressions. Suppose something looks blue to me, I can go on to ask if the object really is blue. Suppose my hand feels hot to me. I can go on to ask if my hand really is hot. But if my hand feels sore, it makes no sense to ask whether my hand is really sore. If it feels sore, it is sore, and that closes the matter. It is the same with aches, tingles, itches and tickles. There is no distinction I can make corresponding to the distinction between 'looks blue' and 'is blue', 'feels hot' and 'is hot'. As we may put it, our sense-impressions reflect or fail to reflect the nature of physical reality. Aches, pains, tingles, itches and tickles may have physical causes, but they do not reflect or fail to reflect physical reality in the way that sense-impressions do.

Since there is a difference between sensations of this sort, and sense-impressions, it might be convenient to restrict the word 'sensation' to these cases, and so make a sharp distinction between sense-impressions and sensations. Or, if this proposal is unacceptable, we might refer to sensations like pain as 'sensations proper.' At any rate, this class of sensations is quite distinct from sense-impressions, and it is not obvious that a discussion of *perception* need pay these sensations anything but incidental attention.

Our discussion of the Argument from Sensation, therefore, has shown the necessity to distinguish between the *sensible qualities* of objects, our *sense-impressions* of objects, and our *sensations* or *'sensations proper'*. Any attempt to identify these three sorts of entity is incorrect.

I should hasten to add that it has not been shown that it is impossible to give an account or analysis of one of these three sorts of thing in terms of the others. For instance, no argument we have advanced *so far* would show it was wrong to give an account of what it is for a thing to have a sensible quality in terms of the sense-impressions the object furnishes to selected observers. To prove that A's cannot be *identified* with B's does not prove that A's are not *reducible* to B's.

Sensations ('sensations proper') have been distinguished only to be dismissed. I believe they have no *special* importance in the

9

discussion of perception, or at any rate in the discussion of the problems we are concerned with. Future references to them will be incidental only. There are many difficult and tangled problems connected with the nature of sensation, but we shall not take the investigation of these problems any deeper in this work.

2. THE ARGUMENT FROM THE RELATIVITY OF SENSIBLE QUALITIES

We pass on to consider an argument to prove that the sensible qualities are subjective which is, if anything, even less convincing than the Argument from Sensation. Once again, however, as we shall see, points of importance do arise out of considering it.

One example of this argument is to be found in Berkeley's *Principles of Human Knowledge* Sec. 11, where he says:

> . . . great and small, swift and slow, are allowed to exist nowhere without the mind, being entirely relative, and changing as the frame or position of the organs of sense varies.

In the 'First Dialogue' Berkeley produces other examples: the mite will see as large what we see as small, what seems hard to one species of animal, may seem soft to another who has 'greater force and firmness of limbs'.[1]

Now we need waste no time in discussing whether or not this argument is valid, for it is obviously not. But it is worth discussing exactly what has gone wrong here.

In the first place, the so-called 'qualities' of greatness, smallness, swiftness and slowness, hardness and softness, etc., are all *relational* properties of objects. To talk of an object as large or swift or hard is to talk elliptically, it is to understand some *standard* of greatness, swiftness or hardness which is not mentioned, but which must exist if our attribution of these 'qualities' is to have any meaning.

Now in a great number of cases, as Berkeley has correctly observed, the standard which is implicitly understood is given by *our own body*. When Achilles calls me a slow runner he means that I am a much slower runner than he, Achilles. When the tortoise

---

[1] Op. cit. pp. 189, 191. Plato produces similar arguments in Book V. of the *Republic*, with the object of proving that physical objects lie half-way between existence and non-existence.

calls me a fast runner he means that I run much faster than he, the tortoise. Our own body is often used as a standard object in this way, both because it is an object that is readily available, and because we are specially interested in our own body. Now, when I perceive an object, I normally not only perceive the object itself, but I also have some perception of my own body, and its relation to the other object perceived. Hence I am able to say 'I perceive it is a large object' meaning that I perceive it is larger than my body. (Of course, I do not always mean this by 'large', I may only mean 'large as objects of that sort go'.)

What Berkeley then does is to pass illegitimately from 'large relatively to me' where 'me' means 'my *body*' to 'large relatively to me' where 'me' means 'my *mind*'. Hence he reaches the conclusion that these 'qualities' are subjective. Once we refuse to make this transition, any puzzle about this sort of case vanishes. The mite sees an object bigger than its body. I see the same object, which is smaller than my body. The mite calls the object large, I call it small, but our remarks pass each other by because we are speaking of relations the object has to different things.

Now the tracking down of the fallacy involved here is important, because it turns out that one of the most hoary and respected puzzles about perception is really a *concealed* example of this same simple mistake. It is traditional to raise problems about the change in the apparent visual size and shape of the objects we see, as we approach to, recede from, or otherwise alter our position in regard to, these objects. Thus Berkeley says in the 'First Dialogue' that:

> . . . as we approach to or recede from an object, *the visible extension varies* [my italics] being at one distance ten or a hundred times greater than at another.[1]

Again, we have been confronted *ad nauseam* with the penny that looks elliptical when viewed obliquely.

Now here we seem to be dragged in two different ways at once. In the first place, it is true that when we approach an object we do want to say that *something* gets larger. Objects do 'loom up on us' as we get closer to them. Again, when we view a round object obliquely there does seem to be some force in saying that *something* elliptical is involved.

[1] Op. cit. p. 189.

Yet at the same time we are driven to say the opposite. When we approach an object, does it normally *look* any larger, even in the strictest and most phenomenological use of the word 'look'? Does the penny normally look elliptical when viewed obliquely? Perhaps such things do happen *in rather special contexts*, but do they invariably happen? Surely it is the exception, not the rule, for something to look larger as we get nearer to it, or for something round to look elliptical when viewed obliquely, even in the strictest phenomenological sense of the word 'look'?

Traditional philosophy has tended to go in the first direction, recent writers have emphasized the second point. A satisfactory solution would do justice to both lines of thought.

I think this antinomy can be resolved if we realise that, when we see an object, normally we can see not only the object but also the relations that our *body* has to the object. When Berkeley talks about the 'visible extension' of a thing varying as we approach to, or recede from, a thing, what he is really talking about is a change in our body's relation to the thing, a physical change that really occurs, which is in no way illusory, and which we can observe.

Suppose that there were an open grille with squares like graph paper set up perpendicularly at a short, but fixed, distance in front of our eyes.[1] Suppose further that lines are drawn from the perceived object to our eyes. These lines will form a pattern on the grille of a certain size and shape. Let us call what is projected on the grille the 'square' size and shape of the object perceived. Now a thing's 'square' size and shape is perfectly objective, and it is not determined simply by the size and shape of the object. Rather it is a function of the object's size and shape, together with the spatial relations that the object has *to our body*. The 'square' size and shape of an object changes as we change our position relative to the object.

Now the 'square' size and shape of a perceived object *has* just those properties which Berkeley and others said that the per-

[1] I have used this device before. Cf. 'Illusions of Sense' *Australasian Journal of Philosophy*, Vol. 33, 1955, pp. 95–97. The account offered by H. H. Price in his article in 'Contemporary British Philosophy' (Third Series) does not use the image of such a grille, but is essentially very similar. Cf. also John Anderson 'The Knower and the Known' *Proceedings of theAristotelian Society*, N.S. XVII, 1926–27, pp. 74–77.

ceived object *looked* to have. As we get nearer an object it is geometrically necessary that the 'square' size of the object increases. If we view a round penny from an oblique angle it is geometrically necessary that its 'square' shape is elliptical. What is more, an object's 'square' size and shape is something that we can and do actually *observe*, just as much as we can observe the *intrinsic* shape and size of the object. The fantasy of the grille is just a device to make the conception of 'square' size and shape more vivid. We can, and do, perceive what is the projected size and shape of a perceived object onto a perpendicular cross-section of the space before our face.

Suppose, then, that two observers are viewing the same object from different positions and at different distances. Unless conditions are very unusual (e.g. unless the object is very distant, at a very unusual angle, etc.) the object will look to both observers to have the intrinsic size and shape that it really does have.[1] But in addition, the two observers will be able to see the spatial relations that their own bodies have to the object perceived, and this means they will be able to see what is the 'square' size and shape of the object relative to their own body. And this 'square' size will be larger the nearer they are to the object, and the 'square' shape will differ according to the angle from which the thing is being viewed. So *something* gets larger when we get nearer to an object we are looking at, and this *something* is elliptical when we view a round thing from an oblique angle. But the presence of this something is perfectly compatible with the thing looking the size and shape it really is, in the strictest and most phenomenological sense of the word 'looks'. Furthermore, the two perception-reports of the two observers in no way contradict each other, nor does any reason appear to treat this 'thing that gets larger' or this 'elliptical thing' as *mind*-dependent, any more than any other feature of the physical environment. We are simply talking about objective spatial *relations* that hold between our body and the object we are perceiving.

So it appears that the argument from the relativity of certain sensible qualities is not merely of historical importance or of

[1] I am simply *assuming* that visual perception is three-dimensional. The Berkeleyan view that the visual field is only two-dimensional receives less and less support nowadays, although it still deserves examination. This, however, we are unable to undertake here.

importance for Berkeleyan scholarship. The same principle that underlies its refutation also underlies an account of the puzzling phenomenon of the *so-called* 'apparent changes of size and shape with the change in the position of the observer'. Once this phenomenon is *correctly described* it is seen to be no more puzzling than the simple difficulties which Berkeley uses invalidly to try to establish the subjectivity of certain of the sensible qualities of things.

3. THE ARGUMENT FROM ILLUSION

The final argument that Berkeley brings to prove the subjectivity of the sensible qualities of things is based on the fact of sensory illusion. In the case of colours, for instance:

> upon a change happening in the humours of the eye, or a variation in distance, without any manner of real alteration in the thing itself, the colours of any object are either changed or totally disappear.[1]

He then draws the conclusion that the colours of objects are all 'merely apparent' i.e. they are subjective. The same sort of argument is also applied to the other sensible qualities.

As it stands, the argument rests on a gross confusion between sense-impressions and the sensible qualities of things. If I look at a white object, but have jaundice, then, Berkeley just assumes, I perceive a yellow object, just as I would perceive a white object if my eyes were normal. But, his argument continues, the yellowness is merely apparent, and so is subjective. But if the perceived yellowness is subjective, so must the perceived whiteness be in the case where my eyes are normal.

Now, of course, this argument simply begs the question, because we do not say that a white wall viewed by a jaundiced man *is* yellow, but only that it looks yellow to him. We distinguish between a wall being yellow (a quality of the wall) and its looking yellow to jaundiced observers (sense-impressions that they have). The fact that sense-impressions are subjective does nothing to show that the qualities of the wall are subjective.

Hence we must reject this third argument as it stands. Nevertheless, this is not the end of the Argument from Illusion. It can

[1] Op. cit. pp. 185–6.

be reformulated in a very persuasive way, not with the direct object of showing that the sensible qualities of objects are mind-dependent, but with the object of showing that the *immediate objects of awareness* when we perceive are not physical existents but are mere sense-impressions. Our next chapter, then, will ask what are the immediate objects of awareness in perception.

PART TWO

The Argument from Illusion

2

WHAT ARE THE IMMEDIATE OBJECTS OF AWARENESS IN PERCEPTION?

WE must begin by elucidating the differences between *immediate* and *mediate* perception, and in order to do this we will consider a passage from the 'First Dialogue':

> ... when I hear a coach drive along the streets, immediately I perceive only the sound, but from the experience I have had that such a sound is connected with a coach, I am said to hear the coach. It is nevertheless evident, that in truth and strictness, nothing can be *heard* but *sound*: and the coach is not then properly perceived by sense, but suggested from experience. So likewise when we are said to see a red-hot bar of iron; the solidity and heat of the iron are not the objects of sight, but are suggested to the imagination by the colour and figure, which are properly perceived by that sense. In short, these things alone are actually and strictly perceived by any sense, which would have been perceived, in case that same sense had then been first conferred on us. As for the other things, it is plain that they are only suggested to the mind by experience grounded on former perception.[1]

In the first place, this passage contains an important mistake. The mistake is Berkeley's inclination to say that we are actually asserting something *false* when we say that we hear a coach or see that a bar of iron is red-hot. In fact, of course, these are very respectable ways of expressing ourselves, and although such state-

[1] Berkeley, Works. Vol. 2. ed. T. E. Jessop, p. 204.

19

ments can be false they can also be true. Despite his promises
elsewhere that he will never quarrel with anybody for a mere
word, Berkeley is at the old philosopher's game of trying to make
us give up, or at least become uneasy about, certain *ordinary ways
of expressing ourselves*. And the point to be made against him is, of
course, that if a form of expression conveys our meaning
adequately it is unclear why we should be forced to talk in another
way.

But under cover of this confusion Berkeley seems to be drawing
a real distinction of the utmost importance. Perhaps his point may
be best put by saying that when we talk about hearing a sound,
and when we talk about hearing a coach, we are using the word
'hear' *in two different ways*. Again, when we speak of seeing the
colour and shape of an object, and when we speak of seeing that
it is red-hot, we are using the word 'see' in two different ways.
But what is the difference of senses here? Well, earlier in the
'First Dialogue' Hylas is made to say:

> in truth the senses perceive nothing which they do not perceive
> immediately: *for they make no inferences.* [My italics.][1]

Following up this hint, let us try saying that, when we hear a
sound, we have *immediate* perception, because there is no *inference* involved; but that when we hear a coach we have only
mediate perception because it involves an inference from the sound
that is immediately heard, to the coach that is not immediately perceived at all. (Let us assume, for the sake of argument, that the
sound that coaches make is in no way part of what it is to be a
coach.)

It is not implied that immediate perception precedes mediate
perception in point of time. In point of time, it seems that the
coach is heard as immediately as the sound. But we can be said to
have heard the coach only because we have heard the sound. We
may not have paid much attention to the sound, we may have been
much more *interested* in the coach than in the sound, but we must
have heard the sound in order to hear the coach. But the reverse
implication does not hold. Somebody who heard a noise, which
was in fact made by a coach, but who was unfamiliar with the
noise that coaches make, could not say that he heard a coach. Or
at any rate he could not say that he knew he was hearing a coach.

[1] Op. cit. pp. 174–5.

20

Immediate perception, then, is perception which involves no element of inference, while mediate perception does involve such an inference.[1] But we have only to propose this definition to see that it is at least dangerously misleading. Berkeley is on stronger ground when he says that mediate perception is a matter of *suggestion*, based on experience. The child immediately perceives the visual qualities of the fire, and is drawn to them. But then he touches the fire and immediately feels the heat, accompanied by a sensation of pain. Afterwards, the immediate perception of objects with similar visual qualities will *suggest* to him that these objects are very hot, and cause pain on contact. But there need be no actual *inference*. It is much more like the association of ideas, as indeed Berkeley brings out by the word 'suggests'. Certain things are immediately perceived, and then we just find ourselves with certain mediate perceptions. We may not even be able to say just what it was that gave rise to a particular mediate perception, and the matter may have to be subjected to an elaborate investigation. (Psychologists, of course, actually concern themselves with this task.)

Immediate perception, then, is perception which involves no element of suggestion. We can say if we like that it involves no element of inference, but we must remember the latitudinarian sense of the word 'inference' that is being employed. But there seems to be a clear and important distinction here, and one well marked by the use of the words 'immediate' and 'mediate'.

Before going on to ask just what *are* the immediate objects of perception, there are one or two points to be made which may cast some further light on the nature of the distinction being drawn. In the first place, there is one remark that Berkeley makes about immediate perception which I think we ought to treat with caution. He says, it will be remembered:

> In short, these things alone are actually and strictly perceived by any sense, which would have been perceived in case that same sense had then been first conferred on us.

This may be a useful remark to make when trying to make clear to somebody what immediate perception is, but it suggests something that may well be false. There is no necessity for our powers

---

[1] 'Inference' here is used in a psychological, not a logical sense. That is, it is not necessarily a *valid* inference.

of immediate perception to remain static. We have good reason to believe that when a baby first opens its eyes, or when a blind man gains his sight, not only is their mediate visual perception non-existent, but their immediate visual perception is vastly inferior to that of the normal adult. As we know, our powers of immediate perception can fail (failing eyesight, increasing deafness), or can improve (some defects of eyesight correct themselves as we get older). It is therefore a matter for empirical investigation just what is immediately perceived by somebody who has just had a sense 'conferred upon him'.

This leads on to the interesting question whether there is an absolutely sharp line to be drawn between immediate and mediate perception. If the head of a cat is poking out from behind a door, then it is clear that to say 'I see a cat' is to speak the language of mediate perception, while to say 'I see a black thing of a certain shape' (a shape like one side of the front of a cat) is to speak the language of immediate perception. But are there perhaps intermediate cases where it is not clear what we should say?

Consider the case where I hear familiar words spoken in a rather slurred voice. Is it clear just what was the immediate object of hearing? Or suppose I look at a full moon on a clear night. Is my immediate perception of the moon a perception of something round, or is it a perception of a flat disc which simply *suggests* to me that I am looking at something round?[1] Here we seem to be in an intermediate region where immediate perception merges into mediate perception, as baldness merges into hairiness. Decision on classification here looks to be no more than a *linguistic* decision. So I think we ought not to commit ourselves to the view that there is a hard and fast distinction between the two sorts of perception.

Corresponding to the notion of immediate perception we have the notion of immediate perceptual illusion. If I see a dummy which has the visual qualities of an orange, and am deceived, I could say I was subject to sensory illusion. But I was certainly not subject to *immediate* sensory illusion. But if I seemed to see an object with the visual qualities of an orange, yet there was really

[1] '"Does the moon look flat to you, or round?" asked Ralph. "I don't know," said the girl sadly, looking at the moon.' (Terry Southern: *Flash and Filigree*.)

22

nothing there *at all*, I would have been subject to immediate perceptual illusion.

This distinction between immediate and mediate perception is central to the argument of this book. As we go on, we will say more about it, and gain a deeper understanding of its nature.

Now, in the example that Berkeley gives, what he *says* to be immediately perceived is a physical event, the occurrence of a certain sound, and we too have accepted this view. But is this Berkeley's considered view? Does he not really think that the immediate objects of perception, those which involve no element of inference or suggestion *at all*, are a man's own sense-impressions? Here we must remember Berkeley's failure to distinguish between the sensible qualities of things and sense-impressions. Elsewhere, indeed, he makes it perfectly clear that, in the case of the coach, he holds that the *real* immediate object of perception is our auditory sense-impression of the sound of the coach. As he frequently observes 'whatever is immediately perceived is an *idea*', that is, a sense-impression.

So it seems that we must make a decision. Do we continue to accept our original view of immediate perception, or do we accept Berkeley's considered view that the objects of immediate perception are always sense-impressions?

Now the answer we give to this question is of the utmost importance, since it serves to mark the distinction between Direct Realism on the one hand, and the Representative and Phenomenalist theories of perception on the other. Direct Realism may be characterised as the view that the immediate objects of perception are physical existents. What we immediately perceive are physical existents of a certain sort. In opposition to this, the Representationalist and the Phenomenalist are at least united on this point, that the immediate objects of perception[1] are sense-impressions. (For our purpose here, Berkeley may be treated, not too inaccurately, as a species of Phenomenalist.)

As we have already noted in the Introduction, there is considerable confusion in modern philosophical thought about the nature of these theories. We sometimes find it asserted that Direct or 'Naïve' Realism is the doctrine that we perceive physical

[1] Some philosophers would substitute the word 'sense' for 'immediately perceive'. But they seem to mean exactly the same thing.

objects, that is, see trees, touch tables and taste food; and that those who uphold a Representative or a Phenomenalist theory of perception are engaged in denying these very obvious facts. The issue, in other words, is represented as the same as the issue between common-sense, on the one hand, and scepticism, on the other.

Now it should be obvious that this is quite wrong. Even Berkeley, who had not been subjected to the formidable barrage of arguments against scepticism which were features of the philosophical work of G. E. Moore and Wittgenstein (each in his own way), is extremely careful to point out that he is not *denying* the existence of physical objects, nor denying that we can *perceive* physical objects. Yet surely there is some opposition between Berkeley's view and that of a Direct Realist? Although they both oppose the sceptic, are they not differing about something else?

The distinction between immediate and mediate perception enables us to understand just what are these differences. Neither Direct Realist, Representationalist or Phenomenalist need deny the obvious, viz. that it is perfectly legitimate to speak of our seeing, touching, hearing, tasting and smelling physical objects. The Direct Realist theory does part company with the other two theories on the question what sort of thing it is that can be *immediately* perceived. It gives a different account of the *primary* objects of perception. It maintains that even what is immediately perceived is something physical.

Now it is sometimes thought that the issue here can be decided quite simply by considering the way we are inclined to talk. We would not naturally say that a sense-impression was a thing that could be *perceived* at all, and so, a fortiori, we should not naturally say that sense-impressions could be *immediately* perceived. We have sense-impressions, we do not perceive them. For, normally, we so use the word 'perceive' that it implies the physical existence of whatever is said to be perceived. When we have had sense-impressions which fail to correspond to reality we say that we *thought* we perceived, or it was *as if* we perceived, but we do not usually say we were actually perceiving.

Nevertheless, I do not think that this argument from language decides the matter. In the first place, language speaks with a rather uncertain voice on this matter. In the second place, the Argument from Illusion can be revived in a much more powerful form, with the object of showing that, despite ordinary language, it would be more accurate to speak of sense-impressions as the immediate objects of perception. The re-formulated argument may be presented in three stages.

(i) *Immediate sensory illusion does occur*

It has been pointed out that this premiss is a stronger one than the argument strictly requires. All that is strictly necessary is that immediate sensory illusion should be possible. Nevertheless, it would be psychologically impossible for the argument to produce any conviction unless it were possible to point to actual cases of immediate sensory illusion.

I become aware of the existence of immediate sensory illusion because, on occasions, there is an incompatibility between what I seem to perceive immediately and what other observers seem to perceive immediately. If there were mere *difference* in different observer's perceptions there would be no necessity to admit that somebody was subject to illusion. There is no reason why two observers should not observe different features of the same object without either observer being subject to illusion. Objects have an indefinite number of characteristics, and perception is a selective affair. We never perceive more than *some* of the features of an object at any one time. Hence there is no reason why two observers should not 'select' different features of the same object. Indeed, since different observers will be differently situated, and will have different physiological and psychological constitutions, such differences in 'selection' are very likely. But we are only forced to admit sensory illusion where the putative perceptions actually *conflict* with each other. (The error of the Argument from the Relativity of sensible qualities could be said to be the taking of certain observations of different observers to be incompatible, and hence 'subjective', when in fact they are merely different. When the mite calls an object large which I call small we are really concerned with different relational properties of the same object.)

This incompatibility of the putative perceptions of different observers serves as a *mark* to indicate the presence of sensory illusion; where such incompatibility occurs at least one of the observers *must* be subject to sensory illusion. For instance, it is sometimes argued that mirror-images are not illusions because they are 'public' objects which can even be photographed. But consider the case where I am two feet in front of the mirror, and looking towards it, while you are looking at the place which is two feet behind the mirror's surface. What I seem to perceive immediately is an object having the same visual qualities as myself (except for the left-right inversion) *but two feet behind the surface of the glass*. Now you are actually looking at the place two feet behind the glass's surface. What you seem to perceive immediately is something that may quite well be incompatible with what I seem to be perceiving. We are therefore forced to conclude that when I look into the mirror I am subject to immediate sensory illusion (an illusion that usually fails to deceive me).[1] I see the world as containing something that in fact it cannot contain.

(ii) *When we are subject to immediate sensory illusion we are immediately perceiving sense-impressions*

Suppose, then, that we do have a case where immediate sensory illusion occurs. Suppose, e.g., I am suffering from auditory hallucinations and I wrongly think I am hearing a sound, or I have an experience as if I were hearing a sound, although there is no sound being made. Now, surely, in some sense am I not *perceiving*? The sound that I hear may not be a physical object. It may be wrong to speak of it as a *sound* or of *hearing* it. But surely it is there in my sensory field? It cannot be conjured away. If we are not allowed to say we hear it we shall just have to find another word. Perhaps we should say that we are aware of it or that we sense it? But the overwhelming resemblance to perception makes it natural to ignore ordinary usage and to talk about perception instead. It is utterly natural to be driven along this path, and so come to say that when we have an auditory hallucination we immediately perceive *an auditory sense-impression*. And so for every other case of immediate sensory illusion.

(iii) *Immediate veridical perception is indistinguishable from immediate sensory illusion*

Somebody who had admitted the second step might still maintain a modified form of Direct Realism. In the case of immediate sensory illusion he would admit that the immediate objects of per-

---

[1] This important point will be fully dealt with in Chapter 7, where it will be shown that, despite the absence of deception, it is quite proper to refer to such 'objects' as mirror-images as illusions.

ception were not physical. But he would continue to maintain that, in veridical perception, the immediate objects of perception were physical existents.

But it seems clear that this compromise is inadmissable. When I suffer auditory hallucination it is logically possible for me to be having a veridical perception of an actual noise. My perceptual experience will be absolutely identical in both cases. Now if it is admitted that in auditory hallucination the immediate object of perception is an auditory sense-impression, and if it is admitted that the very same experience could be a veridical perception, it can hardly be denied that even in veridical perception the *immediate* object of perception is a sense-impression. This result can be generalised to apply to all immediate perception. Whenever I have a veridical perception, it is possible that I should have had exactly the same experience, yet the perception have been illusory. My immediate object of perception in the illusory case would have been a sense-impression, so my immediate object of perception is always a sense-impression.

This is a powerful and a persuasive argument, and it deserves to be taken seriously. So what I will do in the succeeding four chapters is to examine the two theories of perception which come up for consideration once this argument is accepted. We will show that there are decisive objections to both these theories, and this will give us confidence to go back and propose an analysis of immediate sensory illusion which will avoid the necessity of assuming that the immediate objects of perception are sense-impressions.

3

REFUTATION
OF THE REPRESENTATIVE
THEORY OF PERCEPTION

NOW, if it be granted that sense-impressions are the only immediate objects of perception, there are two possible positions
that we can take up about the nature of physical objects. We can
say with Descartes and Locke (and this is the *natural* thing to say)
that physical objects are entities quite other than sense-impressions, but that they somehow give rise to sense-impressions in us.
Alternatively, we can go along with Berkeley and say that physical
objects are nothing but *constructions* out of sense-impressions
(possible sense-impressions perhaps included). And these two
choices define Representationalism and Phenomenalism respec-
tively. Neither view need deny that physical objects exist, or that
they can be perceived, but they take up different positions about
the nature of these objects. They agree only, against the Direct
Realist, that the *immediate* object of any perception can never be a
physical object, or any part or feature of such an object.

Our present concern is with the Representative theory. The
difficulties for this view are so well-known, and are so little a
matter of controversy, that we may set them out briefly. We will
look at three arguments, two of which at least are to be found in
Berkeley's writings. The first of these arguments is familiar to the
point of nausea.

I. WE HAVE NO REASON TO BELIEVE IN THE EXISTENCE OF THE PHYSICAL OBJECTS POSTULATED BY THE REPRESENTATIVE THEORY

It seems clear that we learn of the existence and properties of physical objects by means of our senses. We open our eyes and, as a result of doing this, we perceive a tree. If we had no senses, we should not have been aware of the existence of physical objects such as trees. Now it is clear that an upholder of the Representative theory of perception will have to say that the perceiving of a physical object or event is *mediate* perception based on the *immediate* perception or awareness of a sense-impression. But then the question arises what warrant we have for believing in the existence of these mediate objects of perception. Consider the account that we would *normally* give of 'hearing a coach'. We hear a certain sound, and then we say we can hear the coach. Now we say this because on some previous occasion we have had immediate perceptions of coaches (or, at any rate, immediate perceptions of certain parts and features of coaches); and we have discovered that when such an object is immediately seen moving, then a sound is immediately heard. Mediate perception of physical objects seems to be based on the immediate perception of certain constant connections. It is true that we must not under-estimate the role of the imagination, which anticipates all sorts of connections and regularities in the world on the slenderest basis of experience. But, even so, there must be *some* basis of experience, some immediate perception of certain connections between things, before we can have any warrant for believing in the existence of mediate objects of perception. What is now mediately perceived was once immediately perceived, or something like it was immediately perceived.

Now, if the Representative theory of perception is correct, we have no evidence at all for passing from the immediate perception of sense-impressions to the mediate perception of physical objects. The hypothesis that sense-impressions are caused by physical objects can never be suggested by immediate perception, nor can it be confirmed. This means that we have no good reasons for believing in the existence of physical objects.

Berkeley sums up the position in a masterly way in the *Principles* (Sec. 20), where he says:

Suppose, what no one can deny possible, an intelligence, without the help of external bodies, to be affected with the same train of sensations or ideas that you are, imprinted in the same order and with like vividness in his mind. I ask whether that intelligence hath not all the reason to believe the existence of corporeal substance, represented by his ideas, and exciting them in his mind, that you can possibly have for believing the same thing? Of this there can be no question; which one consideration is enough to make any reasonable person suspect the strength of whatever arguments he may think himself to have for the existence of bodies without the mind.

Substitute the more accurate term 'sense-impression' for 'sensations or ideas', and then, once granted that the immediate objects of perception are never anything but sense-impressions, the 'hypothesis of corporeal substance' is backed up by no evidence whatsoever. It is no good arguing that, since everything has a cause, our sense-impressions must have an external physical cause. For, as Berkeley pointed out, even if we admit the necessity for such a cause, we have not the slightest reason to treat it as a *physical* cause.

It may be replied that all this argument proves is that we cannot have any *inductive evidence* for the existence of the physical world. But it would still be possible that we might *form the hypothesis* of the existence of the physical world; and, having formed it, we might find that it served to explain the regularities and irregularities in the flow of our sense-impressions. In this way it would be indirectly confirmed, although not directly confirmable.[1]

This objection seems just, and blunts the edge of the argument. But it does not turn it altogether. For surely we are not prepared to degrade bodies into hypotheses? We want to say that our assurance of the existence of the physical world is far stronger than any assurance we could obtain by indirectly confirming a theory. If the Representative theory were true, it would be proper to have a lurking doubt about the existence of the physical world. Yet such a doubt does not seem to be proper.

[1] This point was put to me by Mr. F. J. Clendinnen and by Professor J. J. C. Smart.

REFUTATION OF THE REPRESENTATIVE THEORY

2. ON THE REPRESENTATIVE THEORY, THERE CAN BE NO RESEMBLANCE BETWEEN SENSE-IMPRESSIONS AND PHYSICAL OBJECTS

The previous criticism of the Representative theory was so familiar that it was only necessary to gesture at it. We pass on to consider an interesting and little discussed argument by which Berkeley seeks to prove that if there were such objects as the Representationalist postulates, they could in no way resemble our sense-impressions. In the *Principles* (Sec. 8) he writes:

> But, say you, though the ideas themselves do not exist without the mind, yet there may be things *like* them whereof they are copies or resemblances, which things exist without the mind, in an unthinking substance. I answer, an idea can be like nothing but an idea; a colour or figure can be like nothing but another colour or figure. If we look but ever so little into our thoughts, we shall find it impossible for us to conceive a likeness except only between our ideas. Again, I ask whether these supposed originals or external things, of which our ideas are pictures or representations, be themselves perceivable or no? If they are, *then they are ideas*, and we have gained our point; but if you say they are not, I appeal to any one whether it be sense, to assert a colour is like something which is invisible; hard and soft, like something which is intangible, and so of the rest.

The argument is extremely ingenious. We may reformulate it thus. Either it is logically possible to perceive physical objects immediately, or it is not. Now on the Representative theory the only thing that it is logically possible to perceive immediately is a sense-impression, while physical objects are things quite other than sense-impressions. So it is logically impossible to perceive physical objects immediately. But this means that any characteristic that sense-impressions have is a characteristic that physical objects cannot have. For consider the characteristic X which is a characteristic of a certain sense-impression. It must be an immediately perceivable characteristic, because sense-impressions are immediately perceivable. Now, by hypothesis, no characteristics of physical objects are immediately perceivable, therefore no physical object can have the characteristic X.[1]

---

[1] It has been objected to me by Dr. A. C. Jackson that the characteristic X might be an observable characteristic when it qualified sense-impressions,

31

But what characteristics have sense-impressions got? If sense-impressions are taken as the Representative theory of perception wants to take them, as entities which are *perceived*, which indeed are the immediate objects of perception, we can hardly deny that they have characteristics such as being red, noisy, hot, extended, enduring, etc. It follows at once that physical objects cannot be red, noisy, hot, extended, enduring, etc. We shall have to deny that physical objects have any of the sensible qualities.

But once this is established, the question arises what characteristics we can ascribe to physical objects. If we cannot even say they have extension and duration it seems that our knowledge of them is merely negative, they become 'things we know not what'.

An attempt to evade this conclusion may be made by suggesting that physical objects are red, noisy, hot, extended, enduring, etc., in a second sense of these words, a sense inapplicable to sense-impressions. Now I think it is undoubtedly true that in speaking of a red sense-impression and a red ball we are using the word 'red' in two different senses. But an upholder of the Representative theory can gain no aid or comfort from this fact. For, if our immediate acquaintance is with sense-impressions alone, the onus will lie on anybody who says physical objects are quite distinct from sense-impressions, to explain what is meant by ascribing predicates like 'red' or 'round' to physical objects. There seems to be no way of discharging this onus which would allow of any intelligible description of physical objects as they are in their own nature.

It is true that there are some characteristics which cannot be

---

but an unobservable characteristic when it qualified physical objects. Professor D. A. T. Gasking has followed this up by pointing to a case where a characteristic is observable in one context, but unobservable in another. We can say there is an *even number* of apples on the table. Here 'even number' is an observable characteristic of a certain group. We can also say four is an even number. 'Even number' is *not* an observable characteristic of the number four, because the number four cannot be observed.

However, I am not convinced by this example. It is a necessary proposition that four is an even number, but a contingent fact that the apples on the table are even in number. Now it will be a contingent fact that a sense-impression has the observable characteristic X, and a contingent fact that a physical object has the unobservable characteristic X. Under these circumstances, I do not see how the very same characteristic could have two different logical grammars.

32

ascribed to sense-impressions, but which we can ascribe to physical objects. For instance, it seems that a visual sense-impression cannot be described as three feet long, but a physical object can be so described. But how can somebody who holds that the only immediate objects of perception are sense-impressions explain the meaning of 'three feet long' except by reference to sense-impressions of certain sorts? Of the physical object itself we would still know nothing except that it had no characteristic in common with the sense-impressions it caused in us.

It is true that this argument does not strictly prove that the Representative theory is false. But only a sceptic could acquiesce in this conception of physical objects as things of which we have a merely negative knowledge, viz.: that they have no characteristics in common with the immediate objects of perception. If we hold, as everybody does hold, that we have a great deal of positive knowledge of the nature of physical objects, then the Representative theory of perception is refuted.

3. THE CONCEPTION OF A PHYSICAL OBJECT WHICH CANNOT BE IMMEDIATELY PERCEIVED IS ILLOGICAL

We have now looked at arguments purporting to show that, on the Representative theory, firstly we could never have any good reason to believe in the existence of physical objects, and secondly, if they do exist, all we could say about them is that they in no way resemble the objects of immediate perception. But we may go further and raise the question whether it is logically possible for there to be such objects at all.

We shall present the argument in two forms. In the first place, the physical object which it is impossible to perceive immediately must have a certain *nature*. It must be a thing of a certain sort, having certain qualities and not having certain others.[1] These qualities, it will have to be said, are not immediately perceivable. Now, the question may be raised, is it possible for *every* quality of an object to be such that it is logically impossible for the quality to be perceived immediately? There are certain characteristics of objects which might be described as unperceivable, for

---

[1] Cf. Berkeley *Principles* (sec. 76) '. . . it seems no less absurd to suppose a substance without accidents, than it is to suppose accidents without a substance'.

example, dispositions. But we can only attribute dispositions to things on the strength of certain non-dispositional characteristics we take them to have, and the question is whether all these characteristics could be such that they could not be perceived immediately.

Now there may well be qualities of objects that human beings, and other perceivers, are unable to perceive immediately. There is good evidence that dogs can hear sounds inaudible to the human ear, and there may well be qualities that no perceiver at all is capable of perceiving immediately. Furthermore, we could perhaps imagine that all the qualities of a certain object were of this unperceivable sort. But these are all empirical impossibilities, and what is empirically impossible is, *ipso facto*, logically possible. It is quite *conceivable* that we should have an immediate perception of these qualities of objects. But can we understand the notion of a thing none of whose characteristics we can even conceive ourselves immediately perceiving? Surely there cannot be such an object which is logically impervious to direct observation?

What I think is the same argument may be put another way. Immediate perception and mediate perception are correlative terms. We can understand talking of the one only if it makes sense to talk about the other. Now if physical objects are mediately perceived, as ·the Representative theory asserts, then we can only understand this assertion if it makes sense to talk of their being immediately perceived. (Compare 'This is an indirect route to the city.' This makes sense only if it makes sense to talk of a direct route. There may not actually *be* a direct route, but we must be able to understand what it would be like for there to be a direct route.) So it cannot be true, as the Representative theory asserts, that it is logically impossible to perceive physical objects immediately.

It seems, then, that the Representative theory's conception of a physical object involves a contradiction.

4

SOME FEATURES
OF SENSE-IMPRESSIONS

THE next task we have to set ourselves is the refutation of
Phenomenalism. But it will be useful to precede this by discussing
certain properties of sense-impressions. This will help us to understand some of the arguments to be brought against Phenomenalism, and also some later discussions. In this chapter, then,
we will ask two questions about sense-impressions:

1. Can there be sense-impressions that nobody has?
2. Are sense-impressions just as they appear to be?

The second question will occupy most of our time. It subdivides
into two further questions:

(*a*) Can we be mistaken about the characteristics of our sense-
impressions?
(*b*) Can our sense-impressions have unnoticed features?

1. CAN THERE BE SENSE-IMPRESSIONS THAT NOBODY HAS?

Instead of talking about 'sense-impressions', as we have done,
Moore and Russell talked about 'sense-data'. They said that the
immediate objects of awareness in perception were sense-data.
Their reason for using the word 'sense-data' was that they wanted
to leave open the question whether these immediate objects of
perception could exist only when there was a mind to be aware of
them. (The word 'sense-impression' is less neutral in this respect.)

35

Russell, indeed, explicitly committed himself to saying that sense-data could exist 'on their own', and often talked about the possibility of 'unsensed sensibilia'.

The importance of the question for a Phenomenalist is obvious. If physical objects are nothing more than constructions out of sense-data, and if the latter can exist only if there is a mind to have them, then objects that nobody is perceiving can only lead a twilight existence as unfulfilled possibilities of minds having certain sorts of sense-data. This leads to a view of reality which makes the perceiving mind central. Reality is a collection of minds that have certain sense-data. In so far as it is anything more than this, it is the unfulfilled possibility of the minds having other sense-data. But if, on the other hand, there can be unsensed sense-data which do not have a merely hypothetical existence, we can escape the necessity for giving minds such a special place in the world-picture, while still accepting a form of Phenomenalism. Physical objects can be conceived of as collections or 'families' of sense-data. Minds are aware of some of these sense-data, and then we have what is called perception of a physical object. But the vast majority of these sense-data are unsensed, and these constitute the unperceived portions or aspects of the physical world. This seems to do much less violence to common sense than the reduction of unperceived physical objects to unfulfilled possibilities of having sense-data.

Unfortunately for the Phenomenalist, however, it seems that Russell's view can be quite definitely ruled out. We have to remember the way that the expression 'sense-datum' is introduced. It is introduced by reference to the possibility of *sensory illusion*, the possibility that the way a thing appears to the senses is not in fact the way it really is. Whenever it looks a certain way to somebody, whenever it feels, tastes, smells or sounds a certain way to somebody, whether or not it *is* this way, then he is said to be having a sense-datum which *has* those characteristics which the physical world *appears* to have. Sense-data are the way the world looks, feels, smells, tastes and sounds to people. How, then, can they exist independently of a mind which has them? We can, of course, introduce a concept of the immediate object of awareness in perception in a different way. But if we do so we shall not provide what those who introduced the sense-datum terminology wanted to provide, viz. an object of immediate awareness which would exist *even in the case of sensory illusion*, even in the cases where we say it *only* looks as if (feels as if, etc.) physical reality were a certain way. It seems, therefore, that Berkeley was right here, and Russell wrong. The 'esse' of a sense-datum (idea, sense-impression) is 'percipi', that is to say, there can only be sense-data where there are persons to have them. Any problem that this raises for the Phenomenalist he will have to face. We shall therefore continue to talk about 'sense-impressions' rather than 'sense-data' with a good conscience.

2. ARE SENSE-IMPRESSIONS JUST AS THEY APPEAR TO BE?

But granted that if there are sense-impressions there must be somebody who *has* these impressions, can we make mistakes about the nature of the impressions we have? Again, can these impressions have any features of which we are not aware? The orthodox view, to be found in Berkeley and Hume for instance, is that neither of these things is possible. Hume puts the matter with splendid succinctness:

'Since all actions and sensations of the mind are known to us by consciousness *they must necessarily appear in every particular what they are, and be what they appear.*' [My italics.] [1]

At first sight this view, which we will call *Hume's Principle*, is clearly correct. Consider first the question of mistakes. If I look at a certain surface I may be mistaken about the colour it has, but surely I cannot be mistaken about my sense-impression of the colour, about the colour that it looks to me to have? 'It looks blue to me, but is it really blue?' makes sense, but 'It seems to look blue to me, but does it really look blue to me?' seems not to. Of course we can ask 'Does it really look blue to *him*?' for here I can very well be mistaken. We can even ask '*Did* it really look blue to me?', for memory can fail, even memory of the way it looked to me. But it seems unnatural to raise doubts about first person present tense statements about the way a thing looks or feels or smells or sounds. It seems almost equally paradoxical to say that sense-impressions can have features of which we can fail to be aware. To say 'I now think that it then looked to me to have a

[1] *Treatise*, 1, iv, 2. Cf. also Berkeley, *Principles*, sec. 25 and 87, and Introduction, sec. 22.

tinge of grey, although I was not aware of this at the time' seems very strange. Nevertheless, there are considerations which seem to cast doubt on Hume's Principle, and to these we must now turn.

(a) Reasons for thinking we can be mistaken about the characteristics of our sense-impressions

In his book *The Problem of Knowledge* A. J. Ayer brings forward a case which he thinks shows that we can be mistaken about the way things look to us. Suppose we are looking at two lines which are in fact approximately the same length. Suppose I am then asked which of the two *looks* longer to me. It is quite possible that I may be unable to answer with any certainty (and not through any doubts about the meaning of the phrase 'looks to me to be longer'). But then, Ayer argues:

> if I can be in doubt about this matter of fact, I can presumably also come to the wrong decision. I can judge that this line looks to me to be longer than that one, when in fact it does not.[1]

Ayer admits that we could have no direct evidence for having made such a mistake, because we cannot re-inspect our experience. But he says that indirect evidence could be given for believing that a mistake had occurred. I suppose that such evidence would be of some form like this: 'You said that A looked longer than B to you, but everybody else says that B looked the longer, and what is more your retina, etc., was in just that condition that normally obtains when you and everybody else say that B looks longer than A.' In such a case we ought to admit that we had been mistaken about the way it looked to us.

(b) Reasons for thinking that there can be unnoticed features of our sense-impressions

Even more powerful reasons can be brought forward in favour of saying that our sense-impressions can have unnoticed features. We shall look at three arguments.

1. H. H. Price writes:

> If one looks at a brightly luminous object, there is a characteristic series of colour-changes in the resulting after-image. How many of us had noticed these, before we read text-books of physiology

[1] Chap. 2, sec. vi. p. 69.

38

or psychology? I myself, before I read William James, had never noticed that the visual size of an after-image alters very greatly if one projects it first on one's finger-nail, and then on to a distant wall. It is natural to say that physiologists and psychologists have *discovered* some characteristics of after-images which the rest of us had not previously noticed, but can notice now when our attention has been called to them. (Again, how many of us had noticed that we are all colour-blind in the margin of the visual field? It is natural to call this a discovery too.)

But if we deny that sense-impressions have unnoticed features:

> . . . such phenomenonological discoveries are logically impossible. What the physiologist did was to alter these after-images, which were just 'coloured' before or just changed their colour— and also their visual size—in a wholly indeterminate manner; and then, by describing this remarkable fact in print, they induced the rest of us to alter our own after-images in a corresponding manner.[1]

Now there is, of course, an ambiguity in the word 'unnoticed'. It may mean that we have paid *no special attention* to the feature of the sense-impression in question, or it may mean that we have not been aware of the feature in question *at all*. Hume's Principle, I take it, would only be concerned to deny that sense-impressions contained unnoticed features in this second sense. The question is whether the evidence Price brings forward suggests that sense-impressions contain unnoticed features in this second sense. I think Price could fairly argue that it does. It is true that if the nature of my visual field changed magically, so that I was now *not* colour-blind in its margin, I should probably notice that my visual field had changed in some way. But equally it seems likely that I should be unable to determine just what the nature of the change was, although this might be determined by later research. We can therefore fairly say that we usually fail to notice the lack of colour-discrimination at the margin of the visual field, in a sense of 'notice' that would refute Hume's Principle.

2. We shall have to recognise further that if we accept Hume's Principle we must admit a very curious consequence, viz. that at least some sense-impressions are *indeterminate* in respect of at least some of their characteristics.

[1] Review of A. J. Ayer's 'Philosophical Essays', *Philosophical Quarterly*, 1955, p. 274.

Consider the case where I look at a table on which are spilled a large number of match-sticks. (We could have used the traditional example of the speckled hen.) Suppose we now consider, not the matches on the table, but my visual impression of the matches. How many 'sense-impression matches' does my impression contain? Suppose I answer this by saying 'Very likely the same number as there are matches on the table, e.g. 63'. But now we have to remember that we are assuming that our sense-impressions are as they appear to be, and appear to be as they are. Does my visual impression really appear to be a 63-match impression? Well, it might be replied, one might be unable to describe it in such precise terms. But it still presents a perfectly definite appearance to me. If it were to change in any way I would notice that. But suppose I am presented with another array of matches of about the same number. Can I say which of the two *visual impressions* contains the larger number of 'sense-impression matches'? But if (*a*) a sense-impression is just as it appears to be; and (*b*) it has a perfectly determinate nature in every respect, then it ought to be possible to say which appearance is the appearance of the larger number of matches. It seems, therefore, that if we want to say that there is nothing in our sense-impressions that we do not notice, we shall have to admit that in this case our sense-impression is a sense-impression of an *indeterminate* number of matches. So at least some of our sense-impressions will have to be indeterminate in at least some respects.

But this seems to make a sense-impression a most peculiar object, if not a walking contradiction. Surely to be is to be determinate? An army cannot consist of an indeterminate number of men, it must consist of a perfectly definite number, even if we do not know exactly what that number is. Must it not be the same for a sense-impression? Why should sense-impressions be permitted this apparent offence against logic, any more than a physical object? All this seems a good reason for thinking that Berkeley and Hume were wrong when they asserted that our sense-impressions are exactly as they appear to be. It seems that we ought to admit that sense-impressions have features which we do not notice, not just in the sense that we do not make these features the particular object of our attention, but in the quite radical sense that we are unable to notice these features, even when we give the task attention. If we accepted this, and so gave up Hume's maxim, we could assert that sense-impressions were always perfectly determinate.

It may enforce our conclusion here if we look at the disastrous consequences of a doctrine which Berkeley held because he wanted to maintain both that sense-impressions are just as they appear to be, and yet never questioned that they are perfectly determinate. We shall then see still more clearly that it is impossible to hold *both* these views. The doctrine in question is that of the 'minimum sensibile'. In the *Principles* Sec. 124 he argues that our sense-impressions of extension (which he, of course, identifies with extension) cannot be divisible into an infinite number of parts because every part of my 'idea' (sense-impression) must be perceived, and 'I cannot resolve any one of my ideas into an infinite number of other ideas'. Berkeley concludes that sensible extension must be made up of a collection of 'minima sensibilia', visible or tangible points which admit of no parts whatsoever.

It is very easy to see, however, that this doctrine runs into hopeless difficulties. In the first place, we have to meet the difficulties that arise for any theory at all that seeks to divide any extension into a finite number of minima. Since the number is finite we must admit the conception of minima which are *next to* or which *adjoin* each other. (A theory which divides extensions into an *infinite* number of minima or points can avoid making this admission. If there are as many points on a line as there are real numbers between 0 and 1, then no point will be next to any other point.) Consider now three adjoining minima. The middle one must occupy a finite extension, or else the first and the third will be next to each other. But this means that it must have two different sides. But if it has different sides it has parts, which contradicts the hypothesis that it is a minimum. The same difficulty can be put in a different way by asking what is the shape of the minimum. Shape implies size, which implies parts. But if there are only a finite number of minima in a finite extension, they must have some shape.

But this is only the beginning of *Berkeley's* difficulties. The very doctrine that sense-impressions are just as they appear to be, which is one of the premises which forces Berkeley towards the doctrine of minima sensibilia, can be brought *against* it. For when we look at extended things our sense-impressions are not arrangements of discrete minima. Surfaces generally look continuous, and it takes an *a priori* argument to persuade us that they never look so. But this means, on Berkeley's principles, that our sense-impressions of extended objects *are* continuous. They have the characteristics they appear to have. Hence Berkeley is driven into an antinomy: he would have to say that visual and tactual sense-impressions both are, and are not, composed of a finite number of minima.

The source of Berkeley's difficulties is clear, he wants to have it both ways. But if he wants to say that sense-impressions are just as they appear to be, then he will have to give up treating sense-impressions as determinate.[1] Only then can he deny the apparently exhaustive disjunction: either visual (and tactual) sense-impressions are composed of a finite number of minima, or they are infinitely divisible. If sense-impressions are not necessarily determinate in every respect, he can say that they may contain a completely *indeterminate* number of finite parts. He can say, that is, that there is no definite answer to the question 'How many distinguishable parts does your visual sense-impression have?' And if it be felt that this doctrine is too extraordinary to be accepted, then the only thing to do is to give up the doctrine that sense-data are just as they appear to be, and to allow that we are only aware of *some* of their characteristics.

3. The final difficulty that Hume's Principle leads to is the problem about the transitivity of similarity. The problem arises very sharply if we consider the following situation, which can actually occur. Suppose we have three pieces of cloth of very much the same colour, but each slightly different in shade. Suppose furthermore that the three shades can be arranged in a serial order A–B–C, so that A and B resemble each other very closely, and so do B and C, but the resemblance between A and C is rather less close. Suppose, now, I look at A and B and I am unable to distinguish between them in respect of colour, however attentively I regard them when the pieces of cloth are laid alongside each other. It would follow from Hume's Principle that the two sense-impressions were *actually* indistinguishable in respect of colour. Suppose the same thing happens when I lay B and C alongside each other. Now resemblance in a certain defined respect is a

[1] Hume takes the same line and gets into the same difficulties. This stultifies the long and ingenious discussion of space and time in the *Treatise*, Bk. 1. Part II.

transitive relation. If an object P resembles an object Q in respect Y, and object Q resembles an object R in respect Y, then it necessarily follows that P resembles R in that respect Y. It seems, therefore, that I ought to be able to say *a priori* that, under these circumstances, my sense-impressions of A and C will be indistinguishable in respect of shade of colour. But in fact this *need* not be so. I may be unable to distinguish my sense-impressions of A and B (in respect of shade of colour), unable to distinguish my sense-impressions of B and C, and yet perfectly able to distinguish my sense-impressions of A and C. And, on Hume's Principle, if I can distinguish the sense-impressions of A and C in respect of colour, they must have a different colour. So it seems that, with respect to sense-impressions, the relation of similarity in a certain respect is not transitive. This seems very strange. How is it possible for similarity in a certain respect not to be transitive, even in the case of sense-impressions? The only way out of this would be to deny the Humean principle, and to assert that in such a case there must be differences between the sense-impressions of A, B and C which we are not aware of when we have the sense-impressions in question.

However, despite all these very powerful arguments, I am not inclined to give up Hume's Principle. But I am somewhat handicapped because I cannot give my whole answer here, but must wait until a later chapter. What I will do here is, first, to give my reasons for clinging to the Principle. I will then try to answer Price's argument to show that our sense-impressions can have unnoticed features, or at any rate I will offer an alternative analysis of the same facts. I will then argue that we can answer Ayer's argument to show we can be mistaken about the characteristics our sense-impressions have, *provided we allow that sense-impressions can be indeterminate*. This leaves me with two paradoxes on my hands: first, the indeterminacy of sense-impressions; second, the fact that resemblance in a certain respect is not necessarily a transitive relation in the case of sense-impressions. For the present I can only ask that these be accepted to be real characteristics of sense-impressions. In a later chapter (ch. 10), I hope all will be made clear, and it will be shown that, once we understand the true nature of sense-impressions, there is nothing at all paradoxical about these apparently fantastic properties.

My reason for wanting to accept Hume's Principle is simply that the idea of either failing to notice or making mistakes about a feature of a sense-impression seems impossible. Consider the difference between an unnoticed feature of a physical object and an unnoticed feature of a sense-impression. If I fail to notice some feature of a physical object, then it is at least logically possible that somebody else should notice this feature. But if I fail to notice some feature of my sense-impressions, then there is not even the logical possibility of somebody else noticing that feature. The only possible way of getting knowledge of my sense-impressions is for *me* to notice something about them. All other claims about my sense-impressions must be checked by what I notice. If we could give a physiological or a behaviouristic account of our sense-impressions it would be a different matter, but they are part of our *experience*. So unnoticed features of our sense-impressions will be unnoticed aspects of our experience, and I am inclined to say that this involves a contradiction. At the very least we should avoid postulating such unnoticed aspects of experience unless we are absolutely forced to. The same sort of argument applies to the making of *mistakes* about a feature of a sense-impression.

Nevertheless, perhaps we must not ride Hume's Principle too hard. A compromise may be possible. And it does seem that the evidence brought forward by Price pushes us towards *giving a sense* to talk about unnoticed features of sense-impressions. And such talk would be perfectly acceptable providing it were agreed that such 'unnoticed characteristics' were not *features* or *characteristics* in the same sense that noticed features were. An unnoticed feature of a sense-impression, it may be suggested, is nothing more than an unfulfilled possibility of having sense-impressions with certain (noticed) characteristics. We can say that after-images have certain characteristics which are not usually noticed, meaning thereby that, whenever a person pays close attention to his after-images, he attributes certain characteristics to them. Unnoticed characteristics of sense-impressions are permanent possibilities of having certain sorts of impression. In this way, perhaps, we can come to terms with Price's argument, without really deserting Hume's Principle.

We have still to deal with the difficulty raised by Ayer where we hesitate to say which of two lines looks longer to us. Ayer argues that we can come to a decision here, and yet that decision can be wrong. This would imply that it is possible to be mistaken about the way things look to us. The compromise that is possible in the case of unnoticed features of sense-impressions is not available here.

However, we must notice that the hesitation Ayer describes only seems to be possible in a case where the objects in question present very similar appearances. In the example he gives, the two lines look to the observer to be very similar, and even if the observer hesitates to say whether one looks to be longer than the other or not, we can be sure of one thing: they look to be of very much the same length. But is it possible to wonder whether a thing now looks to me to be red or to be green? 'I do not know whether line A or line B looks to me to be longer' may be acceptable, but 'I do not know whether this surface looks to me to be green or looks to me to be red' seems insane.[1] The hesitation that is possible in the first case may lead us to talk of making a mistake about which line looks the longer to us. But in the other case the possibility of such a mistake seems not to exist. 'I thought it looked green to me, but it really looked red to me' is fantastic. And if something looks red to me, but looks green to everybody else, and if my retina and nervous system are in that condition which usually obtains when I and everybody else usually say that it looks green to them, we shall not be tempted to say that it really looks green to me, although I think it looks red to me. We shall simply say that there is an inexplicable lack of correlation between my sense-impressions and normal ones.

The fact is, I think, that in the case Ayer cites, hesitation about which of the lines looks longer to me is only possible because our sense-impression of the lines *is not determinate in this respect*. The hesitation actually reflects a characteristic of the sense-impression; unless we hesitated to say whether A looked longer than B, it would not *be* just that sense-impression. To say 'it appears to me in such a way that I hesitate to say whether A looks longer than B or vice-versa' is actually a correct description of the appearance presented. It would follow, if I am right here, that any 'decision'

---

[1] Of course, there is the peculiar case where I start the car when the light turns to red, reacting to it as to the green light. But I do not think that in such a case we would want to say 'I thought it looked green to me, although it really looked red to me'. It looked red to me, but I *treated* it as if it were the green light.

in such a case about which way a thing looked would be an arbitrary one, and *a fortiori* it would be arbitrary to talk about making a right or a wrong decision. And in fact I think we do treat such decisions as arbitrary, as reflecting the demand for a definite decision, and not as corresponding or failing to correspond to the actual nature of the appearance presented.

It seems, then, that provided we accept the possibility of sense-impressions being indeterminate, we can describe the cases Ayer points to in a different way. And so we will escape the necessity of admitting that we can be mistaken about our sense-impressions. We have still left unexplained the mysterious property that sense-impressions possess of being indeterminate, and the necessity we seem to be under of saying that, with regard to sense-impressions, resemblance in a certain respect is not a transitive relation. But these mysteries will find a solution in a later chapter.

5

REFUTATION OF
PHENOMENALISM (1)

IN late years an indefinite number of refutations of Phenomenalism have been proposed, yet the doctrine still finds its
adherents. However, an extraordinary shyness about accepting the
title of Phenomenalist has become fashionable, although the doctrine itself has been no more than driven underground. What we
commonly find today are 'shame-faced Phenomenalists', who hold
to the main substance of the Phenomenalist position, jibbing only
at a word. In this and the next chapter, therefore, I shall confine
myself to arguments which are either so convincing that they
deserve to be mentioned despite their familiarity, or else are
sufficiently unusual to be a new move in an argument that has
tended to become hackneyed.

But before advancing what I take to be good arguments against
Phenomenalism, I shall indicate briefly two lines of objection
which I take to be invalid.

(1) In the first place it is sometimes objected that Phenomenalism must be false because it is not possible to *translate*
physical-object statements into statements wholly about the sense-
impressions, actual and possible, that observers have or might
have. The objection does not base itself on the length and boring-
ness of the task, or on the inadequacies of our vocabulary. Even if
these objections be waived, it is said, there remains a radical
impossibility of translating the former sort of statements into the
latter. For it is always possible for a physical object to exist, and
yet for it to fail to yield appropriate sense-impressions to suitably

47

situated observers. Given any finite set of sense-impression statements offered as a translation, then it is always possible, if circumstances are sufficiently unusual, for the observer to have sense-impressions other than these, yet for the physical-object statement to be true. (Suppose e.g. his nervous system is in a thoroughly deranged state.) It will then be necessary to include these new sense-impression statements in the proposed translation, which will then swell out *ad infinitum*; or else rule them out by stipulating in the translation that the observer or his environment is in a normal state. But in order to define 'normal state' without circularity, it will be necessary to refer to the *physical* state of the observer or environment. This new physical-object statement would require to be translated into the language of sense-impressions, and the trouble would begin all over again.

Now this objection *might* be a conclusive one if we adopt certain definitions of Phenomenalism. Ayer, for instance, once defined it as 'the theory that physical objects are logical constructions out of sense-data'.[1] And he goes on to say that asserting that physical objects are logical constructions out of sense-data means that any physical-object statement is equivalent to some set of statements about sense-data (sense-impressions).

But why should the Phenomenalist define his doctrine in this way? Phenomenalism is not fundamentally a doctrine of the translatability of certain sorts of statement into certain others, but is a doctrine of the nature of the physical world. For the Phenomenalist, the physical world is nothing more than sense-impressions, actual and possible. In talking of physical objects and in talking of our sense-impressions 'of' them, we are not referring to two distinct sets of entities. But this need not imply any possibility of finding an exact equivalence between physical-object statements and sets of sense-impression statements. The 'fit' between physical-object language and sense-impression language (in so far as the latter exists at all) may be extremely loose. Yet the Phenomenalist contention that we can give an account of the concept of a physical object or event purely in terms of sense-impressions may still be true. The doctrine of 'translatability' is simply a misleading way of putting the point, based on a quite over-simple view of what it is to assert the existence of logical relations between certain sorts of things.

[1] *Philosophical Essays*, chap. 6, p. 125.

Here the much canvassed analogy between the relations of nations to their citizens, on the one hand, and the relations of physical objects to sense-impressions, on the other, seems to cast a great deal of light on the matter. I suppose that nobody would be prepared to assert that a *nation* was anything more than certain very complex sets of relations holding between certain persons. It may be, of course, that these persons are as they are, and behave as they behave, because, among other reasons, they are members of a certain nation. But this is only to say that the nature of these persons is in part determined by the fact that they enter into certain very complex relations with a group of other persons. Granting this, the nation is a complex set of relations holding between a group of persons, whose nature is in part determined by membership of the group. We might also want to include among the terms of the relations not only people but also physical objects (e.g. a certain continent); but with this proviso, we can say that a nation is nothing more than certain relations holding between 'its' citizens. There is a logical link between the existence of nations and the existence of groups of persons interrelated in a certain complex manner. Where the former exists, so must the latter, and vice-versa.

Now this might lead somebody with over-simple views about the way our language works to think that statements about nations could actually be *translated* into statements about the individuals that compose them and the interrelationships of these individuals. But a little reflection will show that this is quite impossible. Consider the statement 'In 1939 Australia declared war on Germany'. What translation can be offered of this statement which will not mention nations, or actions which only nations are capable of, such as declaring war? Well, what actually happened? Perhaps Mr. Menzies and certain other persons took certain actions, giving certain orders and issuing certain statements. But it is perfectly clear that we could understand the original statement even if we did not know what actually happened in Canberra or elsewhere at that time. No doubt Menzies played an important part in the declaration of war, but we could understand the original statement without even knowing that Menzies existed. Nor could we try to improve such a translation by drawing up a long list of circumstances, the occurrence of any *one* of which would be equivalent to Australia's declaration of war. We do not even know how to set about drawing up an exhaustive list of such circumstances. We can say that Australia's declaration of war on Germany logically implies that certain persons standing in a certain relation to a group of others took certain actions ('war-declaring' actions) towards another such group of persons. But we can do little more than this to *characterise* the persons, relations and actions. Translation is out of the question, yet at the same time the concept of a nation is clearly tied to the concept of a group of persons related in a certain way, the 'national' way to put it with unavoidable circularity. Or to put it another way, a nation is clearly a construction out of its nationals.

Now the Phenomenalist can cite this case as a model for the relations of physical objects and sense-impressions. He can agree that there is no possibility, even in principle, of producing a translation of physical-object statements into sense-impression statements. But the example of nations and their nationals proves that this does not refute the claim that physical objects are nothing more than certain interrelated collections of sense-impressions, actual and possible. (Of course, it does not *prove* it either. But the Phenomenalist's concern here is only to rebut an objection, not to prove his case.) It appears therefore that this line of objection does nothing to damage the hard core of Phenomenalism.

(2) There is a second line of objection to Phenomenalism which is even less convincing. It may be argued that physical objects must be something more than sense-impressions actual and possible, because there are certain things that can be said about physical objects which cannot be said about sense-impressions, and vice-versa. For instance, a physical object such as a match-box can be carried about in my pocket, but I cannot carry about a sense-impression, or even a collection of sense-impressions, in my pocket. This is a point that *Berkeley* fails to appreciate when he says (*Principles*, Sec. 38):

> But, say you, it sounds very harsh to say we eat and drink ideas [sense-impressions], and are clothed with ideas. I acknowledge it does so, the word *idea* not being used in common discourse to signify the several combinations of sensible qualities, which are called *things*: and it is certain that any expression which varies from the familiar use of language, will seem harsh and ridiculous. But this doth not concern the truth of the proposition, . . .

But the harshness which Berkeley admits to exist is much harsher than he admits it to be. It *makes no sense* to speak of covering one's body with a sense-impression, or putting it in one's mouth.

But although this is true, it does nothing to cast doubt on the truth of Phenomenalism. The example of nations and their nationals is once again at hand to show that differences in the things we can say sensibly about physical objects and sense-impressions are compatible with the thesis that the former are nothing more than a construction out of the latter. For nations are nothing more than a certain interrelation of their nationals, yet the things that can be said sensibly about nations and their nationals differ greatly. A nation can declare war, its nationals cannot. Nationals can fall in love and get married, nations cannot. And so on. The Phenomenalist, therefore, need not be in the least disconcerted by the fact that what we can say sensibly about physical objects is very different from what we can say about sense-impressions.

We have considered briefly these two possible lines of criticism of Phenomenalism because, although they do not seem to be valid, consideration and rebuttal of them casts some light on the exact nature of the Phenomenalist contention that physical objects are constructions out of sense-impressions.

Phenomenalism, we shall take it, is the assertion that the physical world is a construction out of sense-impressions actual and possible, or is nothing over-and-above sense-impressions actual and possible, in the same sense that nations are constructions out of their nationals, or are nothing over-and-above their nationals.

But before passing on to consider difficulties for this doctrine, we ought to notice briefly the existence of a doctrine which may be called 'Phenomenalism of sensible qualities'. According to this view, to say that a certain physical object is red means that this object would look red to standard observers in standard conditions, but it is then denied that we can give an account of 'physical object', 'standard observers' and 'standard conditions' solely in terms of sense-impressions. So we have a Phenomenalism of sensible qualities combined with a realistic view of physical objects.

The difficulty for this view, however, is that the only way we can discover that observers and conditions of observation *are* standard is by using our senses. But, if we are to use our senses aright, we must have an assurance that the conditions under which we observe the conditions of observation are themselves standard. Hence, in order to avoid a vicious regress, it seems that we shall be ultimately forced to give an account of standard conditions solely in terms of the way things *appear*, that is, in terms of sense-impressions. So it seems that we shall be forced into a *complete* Phenomenalism. The only alternative would be to make the physical world something behind the appearances, something not immediately perceivable. So a 'Phenomenalism of sensible qualities' must lead either to Phenomenalism or to a Representative theory.

In a recent paper, Wilfrid Sellars says that 'x is red = x would look red to standard observers in standard conditions' is a necessary truth, but then goes on to say that this is so:

> *not* because the right-hand side is the definition of 'x is red' but because 'standard conditions' means conditions in which things look what they are.[1]

But if this is the meaning of 'standard conditions' the whole statement shrinks to a triviality that nobody need be concerned to deny whatever their view of perception. In fact, however, the phrase 'standard conditions' involves something more: it involves the notion of *normal* or *usual* conditions. The question must arise, therefore, for Sellars, whether it is a necessary truth that conditions in which things look what they are, are the normal or usual conditions of perception. If this is a necessary truth, he seems to be committed to a 'Phenomenalism of sensible qualities', and so, I have argued, to Phenomenalism or Representationalism. If it is not a necessary truth, the original statement can be accepted, but it seems to have no consequences of interest whatsoever. It is certainly not then a 'Phenomenalism of sensible qualities'

We shall now advance a number of arguments against Phenomenalism.

[1] 'Empiricism and the philosophy of mind' in *Minnesota Studies in the Philosophy of Science* vol. 1, p. 275.

I. THE PHENOMENALIST GIVES UNPERCEIVED PHYSICAL OBJECTS A MERELY HYPOTHETICAL EXISTENCE

It is a familiar reproach to Phenomenalism that it gives unperceived objects nothing more than hypothetical existence, a charge which is denied by some Phenomenalists. We shall argue that the reproach is just.

Let us first run quickly over some familiar ground. If it be granted, as we have argued that it ought to be granted, that sense-impressions or sense-data cannot exist save where there is a mind to have them, an immediate difficulty is created for the doctrine that the physical world is nothing more than our sense-impressions 'of' it. For when nobody is perceiving a particular physical object, nobody is having sense-impressions of that object. It seems then that the Phenomenalist must say that it is logically impossible for objects to exist unperceived, that the notion of unperceived physical existence makes no sense. Yet surely the notion does make sense?

Berkeley tried to evade the difficulty by holding that what we call unperceived objects are actually perceived by the infinite mind of God. This amounts to saying that the phrase 'unobserved physical object' is really an elliptical phrase whose expanded form is 'object unperceived by any finite mind, but perceived by the infinite one'. Now if God exists, and if it makes sense to speak of him *perceiving* objects (a dubious point), then presumably he does perceive every physical event that occurs. But the difficulty for Berkeley is that his position demands that he say that the very meaning of the phrase 'unobserved object' involves a reference to the perceptions of God. Berkeley seems to have accepted this conclusion, and even tries to turn the difficulty to his own advantage by making it a new proof of the existence of God. But it is clear that this is a quite implausible analysis of what we mean when we say that there are objects in the world that nobody ever has perceived or will perceive.

Modern Phenomenalists, therefore, beginning with J. S. Mill, have followed up another line of thought which is also present in a less conspicuous way in Berkeley's writings. They have said that to talk about unperceived physical objects, or about unperceived features of physical objects, is to talk about nothing more than sense-impressions that percipients might have had if circumstances

E

had been different. Unperceived objects are unfulfilled possibilities of having sense-impressions. Suppose I manage to avoid knocking a glass off the table. I can say, nevertheless, and say truly, that if I had knocked it off, it would have broken. I can say falsely that if I had knocked it off, it would have floated in mid-air. Such empirical contrary-to-fact conditional statements are capable of truth and falsity. Hence statements about the sense-impressions I might have had, had other circumstances been different, are equally capable of empirical truth and falsity. Hence we can still make meaningful statements about unperceived objects, and such statements raise a real issue which can be discussed and settled objectively.

Now this account of unobserved physical objects in terms of unfulfilled possibilities of having sense-impressions involves many much-discussed problems, most of which we shall not go into. But the obvious preliminary objection to any such account is that, when we say a certain unobserved object exists, we want to say that it *actually* exists, just as the objects we are perceiving do. Our statement may be true or false, but what it is asserting is not that something has a hypothetical existence as an unfulfilled possibility, but that it exists in the full-blooded sense of the word 'existence'.[1]

In *The Problem of Knowledge* Professor Ayer objects to this criticism, arguing that it is based on a confusion between statements about physical objects and statements about sense-impressions. It is true that when we talk about unobserved objects we are talking about the mere possibility of having certain sense-impressions. But that does not mean that we are talking about the mere possibility of the existence of physical objects. We are talking about the *actual*, not the hypothetical, existence of certain unobserved physical objects, and we are saying that what it means to assert the actual existence of such objects is that there are certain unfulfilled possibilities of persons having sense-inpressions. It is not that actual physical objects are reduced to hypothetical physical objects, but that actual physical objects are reduced to hypothetical sense-impressions. Once we distinguish clearly between physical objects and sense-impressions, the criticism fails.

[1] This is the line taken by Isaiah Berlin, 'Empirical propositions and hypothetical statements', *Mind*, vol. LIX, no. 235. Berkeley's account of unobserved objects in terms of the *actual* perceptions of God at least avoids this criticism completely. So does a doctrine of 'unsensed sensibilia'.

This failure to distinguish has arisen, Ayer suggests, because there is no clear 'picture' associated with Phenomenalism in the way that there *is* a picture associated with the Representative theory and with Direct Realism. The Representative theory gives us the picture of the world hidden behind our sense-impressions of it. Direct Realism gives us the picture of the world lying open to our gaze. But, Ayer argues, Phenomenalism gives us no such picture to work with. We cannot picture an unfulfilled possibility of having sense-impressions.

Ayer seems to be completely wrong here. There is a picture associated with Phenomenalism, a picture which is inevitable, and a picture which seems a good reason for abandoning the doctrine. The picture is this: the physical world consists of the sense-impressions that percipients have, *and nothing else at all*. To this it may be objected 'What about the possibilities of having further sense-impressions?' But these are mere unfulfilled possibilities, mere potential existences, and in default of a Leibnizian doctrine of 'possible worlds', or an Aristotelian doctrine of potential being, we cannot treat an unfulfilled possibility as any addition to the sum of things. Consider my desk. It has not been burned up, otherwise it would not still be here. But if anybody had taken a blow-torch to it at any period of its history it could have been burned. Following Mill, we might say it is a permanent possibility of combustion. But we do not think of this unfulfilled possibility of combustion as something over and above the actual desk. This point comes out most clearly if we consider the state of the world before percipients existed. If the Phenomenalist is correct, then, before there were minds having sense-impressions, there was just nothing. You can say 'There were physical objects', but if this only means that there were unfulfilled possibilities of having sense-impressions, that if a mind had existed it would have had certain sense-impressions, this does not contradict the statement that there was nothing.

The objection to the Phenomenalist account of unperceived objects, then, is not just that the Phenomenalist is trying to reduce actual but unobserved physical objects to mere unfulfilled possibilities of the existence of objects. The objection is an objection to the attempt to reduce unperceived physical objects to *anything* merely hypothetical.

What sort of answer can the Phenomenalist make to these

charges? He could evade them completely if he could show the possibility of there being sense-impressions that nobody has (unsensed sensibilia). But for the reasons advanced in the last chapter I do not think that this is a possible way out. The notion of a sense-impression or sense-datum is introduced by reference to the way things appear perceptually to *people*, and cannot be detached from this method of introduction. So I think that all the Phenomenalist can do is accept the strange picture of the world which makes minds and their sense-impressions the only inhabitants of it. (This is Berkeley's picture, although he adds the mastermind of God.) In the ordinary sense of the word 'nothing' there is nothing more in the Phenomenalist world, for unfulfilled possibilities are nothings. If the Phenomenalist is prepared to accept this world-picture I do not think that this present line of argument can be taken any further. But it is a strange view of the world he is accepting.

2. THE PHENOMENALIST MUST ADMIT THAT A UNIVERSE THAT CONTAINS NO MINDS CONTAINS NO MATTER EITHER[1]

Even if we waive this first criticism of Phenomenalism, reflection on the logical properties of empirical contrary-to-fact conditional statements may bring to light further difficulties. Here we shall examine one such difficulty.

Given the truth of some 'open' universal statement about actual things or happenings, we can infer the truth of certain empirical contrary-to-fact conditional statements. Given that all unsupported bodies in the past, present and future fall, then we can infer that if, contrary to fact, a particular body X had not been supported, it would have fallen.[2] In general, given that there are A's, and that every A is a B, we can infer that if, contrary to fact, a particular object or happening X was of the sort A, then it would also be of the sort B.

Contrariwise, given the truth of an empirical contrary-to-fact conditional statement, then we can infer that some 'open' uni-

---

[1] My argument here is inspired by a similar line of thought worked out by Dr. C. B. Martin.

[2] Of course, the sort of statement that we are usually given is only 'Under normal circumstances, unsupported bodies fall'. But we can still derive weaker contrary-to-fact conditional statements from this weaker statement.

versal statement about actual things or happenings is true. It is
true that the situation is a little more complicated than in the case
of the inference from 'open' universal statement, about actual
things or happenings to contrary-to-fact conditional statements.
For given that, if, contrary to fact, a certain object or happening X
had been of the sort A, then it must have been B, we can infer that
all A's are B's. But we cannot infer that there are A's. For instance, we know that if there had been a full-scale atomic war in
1959, the destruction would have been tremendous. But we cannot infer from this piece of knowledge there have been or will be
such wars. However, we could not have asserted this empirical
contrary-to-fact conditional statement unless there *were* 'open'
universal statements about actual things and happenings from
which the proposition 'In full-scale atomic wars the destruction is
tremendous' could be deduced. Whether these relations between
'open' universal statements about actual things, and empirical
contrary-to-fact conditionals, are *entailments* or not, we need not
argue here. But we are entitled to draw inferences from one to the
other, and vice-versa, an inference that does not depend on any
additional suppressed premiss.

Let us now consider the possibility, which seems an empirical
one, that the universe contains no sentient creature in the past,
present or future. Modern phenomenalists generally accept this
possibility that the universe may have contained no sentient
creatures. But they say that this gives them no particular difficulty,
because they can give an account of the things and happenings in
this universe in terms of empirical contrary-to-fact conditionals
about the sense-impressions of sentient beings. If there were sentient beings, they would have sense-impressions of a certain sort.

But the Phenomenalist will have to allow that he can make no
true statements about *any* actual happenings or things in this 'no-
mind' universe. For apparently categorical statements about
physical things or happenings all dissolve, according to him, into
statements about the possible sense-impressions of observers who
do not exist.

This means that the Phenomenalist can make no true 'open'
universal generalisations about anything actual in this 'no-mind'
universe. But, if this is so, he must draw the consequence that he
can make no true empirical contrary-to-fact conditional statements about this 'no-mind' universe either, for their truth depends

on the truth of 'open' universal generalisations about actual things or happenings. But this means, for the Phenomenalist, that no statement about unobserved physical happenings can be true for this universe, for all statements about unobserved physical happenings must be analysed in terms of empirical contrary-to-fact conditional statements about perceptions of observers. This means that the Phenomenalist must infer that in a universe with no minds *there would be no matter either.* Yet, surely, matter can exist in the absence of mind?

The argument may be put briefly. The nature of the merely empirically *possible* is determined by what is *actual.* For the Phenomenalist, in a 'no-mind' universe nothing is actual, therefore nothing is empirically possible, therefore nothing exists at all.

Strictly, this argument does not refute the Phenomenalist. He can simply accept its conclusions. But it is a conclusion that the modern Phenomenalist is not likely to relish.

3. PHYSICAL OBJECTS, WHICH ARE DETERMINATE, CANNOT BE CONSTRUCTIONS OUT OF INDETERMINATE SENSE-IMPRESSIONS

The next argument that we shall consider is based on the premiss, discussed in the previous chapter, that sense-impressions are, at least sometimes, indeterminate. We saw that this follows from the acceptance of Hume's Principle, as we have called it, that sense-impressions are just as they appear to be.

A Phenomenalist holds that a physical object is a collection or family of sense-impressions, viz. all those sense-impressions, actual and possible, which we would normally say are sense-impressions 'of' the object. These sense-impressions will differ widely among themselves, varying with the standpoint and constitution of the observer, but they will all occur in the same context of experience,[1] and will have certain 'family resemblances' to each other. Certain sense-impressions 'of' the object, viz. those obtainable by 'normal' observers in 'typical' or 'standard' conditions[2] are of

---

[1] It is, of course, a problem for the Phenomenalist whether he can give an account of the notion of the 'context of experience' purely in terms of sense-impressions, but this problem, which has received so much attention in recent philosophy, I will leave aside.

[2] Once again these phrases raise familiar difficulties for Phenomenalism, but difficulties which I will not insist upon in this study.

special importance here, and the properties of these sense-impressions, it is said, are what we call, or tend to call, the *real* properties of the physical object.

Now a sense-impression may be indeterminate in some respect, it may be light blue but no definite shade of light blue, it may contain parts but no definite number of parts, and so on. But a physical object is determinate in all respects, it has a perfectly precise colour, temperature, size, etc. It makes no sense to say that a physical object is light-blue in colour, but is no definite shade of light-blue. Now the problem for the Phenomenalist, who treats a physical object as a construction out of sense-data, is whether indeterminate sense-impressions can serve to construct determinate physical objects.

Consider the perception of a line of a certain length. The normal human perceiver will be able to discriminate in respect of length between this line and others which differ slightly in length. Yet it is certain that we could produce lines which were slightly different in length, but which could not be discriminated by such a perceiver. In other words, his sense-impression of the line is in some degree indeterminate with respect to length. Now, by hypothesis, it is a physical object we are dealing with, and so it must have a perfectly determinate length. But if our sense-impressions of the line are always in some degree indeterminate in this respect, how can we say that the physical line is a construction out of sense-impressions? How can the determinate be a construction out of the indeterminate? The same problem will arise with other characteristics of physical objects, e.g. shape or colour or temperature.

The Phenomenalist, I suppose, will try to solve the problem in the following way. When I have a veridical perception of a physical object, yet this perception is indeterminate in some respect, he will say there is at least an unfulfilled possibility that I or other perceivers should have sense-impressions 'of' the same object which would be indefinitely more determinate than our present indeterminate sense-impression. A determinate physical object is a collection of sense-impressions, possible or actual, and included among these sense-impressions are ones having *every possible degree* of determinacy. (Whether a completely determinate sense-impression is or is not a possibility is a question we need not discuss here. The Phenomenalist need only assert that the 'family' of sense-impressions which constitutes a physical object contains sense-impressions of every possible degree of determinacy. He can afford to leave the question open whether any sense-impression can ever be completely determinate.)

At this point a difficulty may be proposed. It is a logically necessary truth that if a physical object exists it is determinate in all its characteristics. But is it not a mere contingent fact that a 'family' of sense-impressions can be found which exhibits every possible degree of determinacy with respect to each characteristic of the object? Is it not perfectly possible that we might find a family of sense-impressions which did not contain sense-impressions having every possible degree of determinacy?

The Phenomenalist's line of reply to this objection is, however, clear. Such a 'broken' family of sense-impressions is, he will agree, perfectly possible, perfectly conceivable. But, he will reply, it is still true that a *physical object* must be determinate, because if such a 'broken' family of sense-impressions were to exist we simply should not count it as a physical object. It is one of the criteria which a sense-impression must satisfy if we are to count it as a sense-impression *of* a physical object, that it belong to a 'family' of sense-impressions which is not 'broken' in this way. The logical necessity of a physical object being determinate no doubt reflects certain empirical facts, in particular the fact that, wherever we have sense-impressions which fulfil the other requirements for being perceptions of a physical object, we can also go on to have sense-impressions of greater and greater determinacy. But this does not mean that there is any logical necessity for such sense-impressions to occur.

It must be allowed that this is a satisfactory answer to the objection proposed. But a new objection may now be brought forward against the Phenomenalist's analysis which is not so easily rebutted. If the Phenomenalist view is correct, to say that a physical object must be determinate is simply to mention one of the tests that a group of sense-impressions must pass before we say that to have one of this group of impressions is to perceive a physical object. Now where there is a multiplicity of tests which an entity must pass in order to be ranked in a certain class, there is always the possibility of modifying our concept of the entity by dropping one of the tests. And in certain circumstances this will actually be done. The question then arises whether we could not conceive ourselves willing to drop this particular demand, and so treat certain families of sense-impressions which did *not* include sense-impressions of all possible degrees of determinacy as being physical objects nevertheless.

And here it seems to me that we are in the grip of a very deep necessity indeed to treat physical objects as being absolutely determinate in every respect. To withdraw this stipulation seems like giving the concept of a physical object a wound from which it could not recover. If this stipulation goes, the notion of a physical world cannot survive. Yet, if we accept the Phenomenalist analysis of what it is for a physical object to be determinate, we are not able to understand why this conceptual demand has such urgency. Why should we not relax our demands a little, and treat as a physical object an orderly and coherent set of perceptions but a set which does not necessarily include sense-impressions of every possible degree of determinacy in every respect? Unless the Phenomenalist can explain our unwillingness to do this, his explanation of what it is for a physical object to be determinate is unsatisfactory.

6

REFUTATION

OF PHENOMENALISM (2)

A PHYSICAL object occupies a certain position in public space, and a certain point in public time. What account can the Phenomenalist give of public space and time? The Phenomenalist is committed to treating the physical world as a construction out of sense-impressions, and it is clear that the construction of a 'public' space and time is simply one aspect, even if a central aspect, of this problem. Let us consider the question of space first. It is clear that the Phenomenalist must say that the individual builds up his concept of space from his visual and tactual sense-impressions. The immediate objects of vision are related to each other by visual spatial relations in the visual field. Tactual experience is an obscure matter, but there seems to be some immediate experience of tactual spatial relations. Beginning with these primitive spatial experiences we can go on to correlate spatially: visual experiences with visual experiences, tactual experiences with tactual experiences, and visual with tactual experiences. When these correlations are eked out by anticipation of further correlations, and by the work of the imagination in 'filling in gaps', the individual has begun to build up something that approaches the single space in which all physical objects have a position.

But even if we admit that all this is possible (which is a question

I do not want to debate), there still remains something missing from the Phenomenalist account. However elaborate a construction the individual may build up out of his primitive visual and tactual spatial experiences, we have to remember that space is something public, that the positions and spatial relations assigned to physical objects do not depend on the individual alone. If his 'construction' clashes with the 'constructions' of other people, then his construction is not *space*. Here, of course, we are simply making a point about space that the Phenomenalist must make about every characteristic of physical objects. For he holds that a physical object is a construction out of the sense-impressions, actual and possible, of people generally. It is only on the basis of a general agreement between the visual and tactual sense-impressions of different people that we can assign position and spatial relations to a physical object.

But now the question arises: What is the nature of the relations that hold between one person's perceptions of an object and another person's perceptions of the same object? What is it that unites a certain collection of sense-impressions of different people, making them all perceptions of the very same object? Now here it is vital to realize that, although the physical object has a spatial position and has spatial relations to other physical objects, the relations holding between different people's sense-impressions of the same object *cannot be spatial relations*. In one sense of the word 'spatial' I can speak of the spatial relations of one of my sense-impressions to another, for example, two different colour patches that occur in my visual field at the same time. In another sense of 'spatial' I can speak of the spatial relations of one physical object to another physical object. But I cannot speak of the spatial relations of my sense-impressions to your sense-impressions: they do not stand in a certain spatial relation to each other in a visual or tactual field, nor are they spatially related in physical space. This is a point that may be concealed, because, when we speak of the physical world as a construction out of sense-impressions, we tend to think of a physical construction, like a house, which involves certain things like bricks and mortar standing in *spatial* relations to each other. But, as we pointed out at the beginning of the previous chapter, to say that a physical object is a construction out of sense-impressions is a very different matter.

Well, what *are* the relations that hold between different people's

sense-impressions of the same object? I think they may be classified under two heads only. One very important relation is *resemblance*. The group of sense-impressions that go to make up one
thing must resemble each other closely. The resemblance cannot
be complete, because, as we know, when different perceivers perceive the same thing, their sense-impressions exhibit differences as
well as resemblances. But there will have to be a family resemblance among the sense-impressions of different people, if we are
to count them as sense-impressions of the same object. If nobody's
sense-impressions ever showed any great resemblance to anybody else's, then, the Phenomenalist would be forced to say,
the concept of the physical world could not have any possible
application.

But although resemblance is clearly necessary, equally clearly it
is not sufficient. For two people could have very similar sense-
impressions, just the sense-impressions that they would have if
they were perceiving the very same object, and yet be perceiving
numerically different objects. (Consider the case of two people
seeing the same film in different cinemas.)

However, besides having relations of *resemblance*, sense-impressions are also *temporally* related. I can have certain sense-impressions before, after, or at the same time as, you have certain sense-
impressions. So if two persons have just the sense-impressions
they would have if they were perceiving the very same object, yet
have these sense-impressions at different times, they are perceiving
different things or different phases of the same thing. (This statement would need to be corrected to allow for such things as the
finite speed of light, but such corrections seem to present no difficulty in principle.)

It may still be objected that it would be possible for two people
to have just the sense-impressions that they would have if they
were perceiving the very same object, have them at the same time,
and yet be perceiving objects at different places. (The same film
shown in different cinemas simultaneously.)

This objection is valid, and illustrates the difficulty the Phenomenalist labours under in having to analyse the notion of 'at a
different place' in terms of sense-impressions, which are not the
sort of things that can be located. But I suppose that the Phenomenalist could say that, where two people have just the same
sense-impressions that they would have if they were perceiving the

very same object, and have them at the same time, we only say they are perceiving two different things when the *preceding* and *succeeding* sense-impressions of the observers are quite different. But if our experience (or our possible experience) did not exhibit significant differences before and after, there would be no reason to talk of the two perceivers perceiving different objects.

So it seems that, although there are difficulties, the Phenomenalist can make some fist of showing how the (public) world of physical objects can be treated as a logical construction out of everybody's (private) sense-impressions. These sense-impressions of different perceivers cannot be spatially related to each other, but they can *resemble* each other, and they stand in *temporal* relations to each other. And these relations may suffice to give an account of the world of spatially related physical objects.

Now up to this point we have talked about time in a quite uncritical fashion. We have simply assumed that it is possible to correlate the sense-impressions of different observers by temporal relations. And there certainly does seem to be a difference between space and time here. While it makes no sense to speak of the spatial relations of my sense-impressions to your sense-impressions, it is perfectly sensible to say that I have a certain sense-impression at the same time as you have another sense-impression. But, nevertheless, there is a problem here for the Phenomenalist, a problem which tends to be ignored. Phenomenalists have been well aware that they cannot simply assume the existence of a single public space in which physical objects are located, but must exhibit space as a construction out of everybody's visual and tactual sense-impressions. But they have tended to assume quite unthinkingly that there is a single public time, and that there is no problem in talking about the temporal relations that hold between different persons' experiences. Yet our immediate experience of time, on the Phenomenalist view, can only be the succession of our own sense-impressions. The question therefore arises how the Phenomenalist can reach the conception of an objective temporal order of events in the physical world.

It might be thought that there is no special problem here. As we have already noted, it is perfectly sensible to speak of the sense-impressions of different perceivers occurring at the same time. Suppose one perceiver has a sequence of sense-impressions of a certain sort: s_1, s_2, s_3. Suppose other perceivers have very similar sequences of sense-impressions, and suppose that these sequences occur at the same time as the original sequence. Then, since all perceivers agree in these sequences, we can say that this is the public order of events. And even if one perceiver has a sequence of sense-impressions which quite fails to agree with the majority, this will not make us deny that the sequence which the majority have is the public order of events. We shall simply say that the minority-sequence is an *illusory* sequence. All this is a mere sketch which would need a great deal of filling in; but, the Phenomenalist might say, it shows there is no difficulty in principle in seeing how the public order of events can be constructed from the private sequences of each individual.

But now let us look at these temporal relations that hold between the experiences of different individuals. Suppose, for instance, that I have a sense-impression as of a lightning-flash, at the same moment as you have a sense-impression as of a thunderclap.

What does '*at the same moment*' mean here? It does not refer to a sense-impression of mine or a sense-impression of yours, for neither of us can immediately perceive the sense-impressions of the other. It must mean that there is an objective relation of simultaneity holding between the occurrence of the two sense-impressions. They occur simultaneously in public time.

So it seems that the attempt to build up public time out of the succession of the experiences of individuals covertly appealed to objective, public, temporal relations to marry together the private experiences. If the Phenomenalist is to proceed in an honest manner, he must build up the conception of public time without appealing to temporal relations holding between the experiences of different minds. For they are part of what has to be built up.

So, in his attempt to give an account of public time, the Phenomenalist can only appeal to relations of *resemblance*. If my sense-impressions 'fit in' with your sense-impressions, in the way that they do fit in when we are in the same place at the same time, then that, he will have to say, *constitutes* being at the same public place and time. To say we exist at the same time simply means that our sense-impressions resemble in a certain way.

It might be thought that the Phenomenalist can argue in the following way. We have certain sense-impressions which can be best explained on the assumption that there are other minds besides our own. I have certain auditory sense-impressions which are best explained on the hypothesis that there is somebody speaking to me now. So it is reasonable to assume that there are other beings who exist at the same time as myself.

But, granting the reasonableness of the assumption that there are other minds, the question is not 'What reason have we to think that there are other minds that exist at the same time as our own?', but 'What do we *mean* by saying that another mind exists at the same time as our own?' The simultaneity in question cannot be the perceived relation of simultaneity that holds between two of our own sense-impressions. It must be objective simultaneity in public time. But this only renews the question 'What can the Phenomenalist *mean* by public time?' And it seems that the only answer that can be given is in terms of the resemblance of the impressions of different minds. Minds whose sequences of impressions 'fit in' in the right way, exist at the same time *ipso facto*.

Now if the Phenomenalist is prepared to hold fast to this doctrine it may not be possible to refute his view. But he is giving an extraordinary account of the nature of public time. When I say I have two different sense-impressions simultaneously, and when I say that you are having certain sense-impressions simultaneously with mine, I seem to be using the word 'simultaneous' in exactly the same sense in each case. Yet the Phenomenalist will have to say that, in the second case, when I refer to the temporal relations of my experiences to your experiences, we are simply talking about the resemblances or 'fit' between my sense-history and yours. If there was no such 'fit' between anybody's sense-history, the concept of public time would have no possible application. This is an incredible view of the nature of public time.

5. PHENOMENALISM CAN GIVE NO ACCOUNT OF THE NUMERICAL
DIFFERENCE OF DIFFERENT MINDS THAT EXIST AT THE SAME TIME

In order to understand the next objection we shall bring against the Phenomenalist, let us begin by discussing our ordinary criterion for numerical difference. What makes two different physical objects that exist at the same time *two*? What is the 'principle of individuation' of physical objects that exist at the same time? It is certainly not a difference in *nature* because, although two numerically different objects that exist at the same time normally differ in nature, yet it is at least logically possible for them to have identical characteristics. What does make the two physical objects two is *occupation of different places*. Consider two billiard balls which exist at the same time. They are numerically different, they are *two* balls, because they are in different places. This may be made clear by a simple thought-experiment. Suppose the two balls approach each other, and then they coalesce magically so that they occupy exactly the same space. In such a case, we will then say that there are no longer two balls, but only one. A thing occupies a certain region of space, different things occupy different regions.

But what constitutes the numerical difference of different *minds* that exist at the same time? This is a more complex question, and I think the answer to it depends on the view we take of the relations of mind and matter. If we accept Analytical Behaviourism (or any other form of Behaviourism), then the problem is easily solved. A body that acts or is disposed to act in a certain way is a body with a mind: a mind is simply a physical qualification of a certain physical substance. On this view, the numerical difference of two minds, however alike, is secured by the spatial separation of two physical objects, the two bodies in question. It is possible, of course, to reject Behaviourism while still taking the mind to be a qualification or predicate of some sort, a non-physical predicate of the body, and perhaps that is one of the things that Aristotle is doing when he describes the mind as the *form* of the body. But in this case, too, the individuation of two minds will be secured, however alike they might be in their mental qualities, by the spatial separation of the bodies they qualify.

But if we accept the Dualist view that minds are quite distinct from the bodies they are associated with, the individuation of different minds that exist at the same time is not such a straightforward matter. Let us suppose that there are two minds which exist at the same time and which have completely similar qualities and experiences. This seems a possible supposition. Now if we accept the Dualist view, on what basis can we say that there are *two* minds here, and not just one? There is no difference in place to individuate the minds, for, on the Dualist view, minds do not occupy a place, or even qualify a spatial thing.

Even here, however, it may be possible for the Dualist to

appeal to the numerical difference of the two *bodies* that the minds are associated with, to solve the problem. It seems reasonable for him to assume that there is a special relationship holding between my mind and a particular body, which makes it *my* body. Now, the Dualist might argue, my mind is the one that has this special relationship to *this* body, another mind is one that has this relationship to *another* body. The two bodies are numerically distinct, so that the minds to which they have the body–mind relationship will be differentiated by their connection to the two different bodies.

Now I do not know if this solution is really adequate for the Dualist. For instance, it might be argued that, in the case of minds that have exactly the same experiences, there would be no telling whether there really were two minds each having a special relationship to a body, or whether there was just one mind that has this relationship to two bodies. I do not know whether this question could be settled. But at least the Dualist could attempt some sort of answer to the question 'What is it that individuates numerically different minds that exist at the same time?'

But now let us consider the position of the Phenomenalist. How does he individuate two different minds? He can make no appeal *at all* to the criteria for the numerical difference of bodies. For if the physical world is simply a construction out of sense-impressions there can be no question of an independently existing physical object (our body) which can help to individuate different minds. Suppose, as seems perfectly possible, that two different minds exist at exactly the same time, and that they have exactly similar experiences, including exactly similar sense-impressions.[1] Now, if Phenomenalism is true, what is there that makes these two minds *two*? We cannot appeal to the numerical differences of bodies in any way, for the bodies dissolve into sense-impressions which are part of the experiences of minds. There seems to be no criterion for numerical difference available.

The Phenomenalist might reply to this by saying that, in such a case, there just is a simple numerical difference, a difference that is not a difference of place. This seems to be an *ad hoc* piece of postulation, and its implausibility may be brought out by asking how any particular individual would come to *grasp* the notion of this

[1] I ignore the difficulties for Phenomenalism over the question of public time, dealt with in the previous section.

sort of numerical difference. Surely one could only do this if one were directly acquainted with two different minds, and so had acquaintance with their principle of individuation? But most Phenomenalists, I suppose, would deny that we did have such direct acquaintance with other minds. It must be admitted, however, that if a Phenomenalist were sufficiently hardy to take such a line his position cannot be formally refuted. We can only point to its implausibility.

There is a second way out of this difficulty that the Phenomenalist might take. He might assert the logical necessity of the Identity of Indiscernibles, that is to say, he might argue that there cannot be two things in the universe that have exactly the same properties. This would mean that there could not be two minds whose *only* difference was a numerical one. If the Phenomenalist is prepared to embrace, and to argue for, this doctrine, our fifth objection loses force. But there are serious objections to maintaining that the Identity of Indiscernibles is a logically necessary truth, although it would take us too far out of our present path to bring forward these objections.

6. PHENOMENALISM CAN GIVE NO SATISFACTORY ACCOUNT OF THE NATURE OF A MIND

We come now to our final, and I think the most telling, criticism of Phenomenalism. It will be a help in understanding the line of argument if we begin by considering what Berkeley says about the relationship of 'ideas' (sense-impressions, sensations and mental images) to the mind. Berkeley is always saying that ideas are 'in' our mind, which of course suggests that he thinks they are part of the mind, or that they qualify the mind in some way. On certain occasions, however, he makes it perfectly clear that this is not his meaning. In the *Principles*, Sec. 49, for instance, he considers the objection that if sensible extension is an 'idea', and so in our mind, this will imply that the mind is extended. And he answers this by saying that sensible qualities such as extension:

> are in the mind only as they are perceived by it, that is, not by way of *mode* or *attribute*, but only by way of *idea*.

Here Berkeley is saying that by 'in the mind' he means only 'is perceived by the mind'. Elsewhere he tells us that a mind, self or spirit is not an idea, or a collection of ideas, but a simple, indivisible, active being quite distinct from its ideas.

Now such a conception of the mind was not likely to survive long in an Empiricist climate of thought. When thinkers like Hume turned their sceptical gaze on themselves, they could not perceive any simple indivisible object which might be identified as the soul or self. Hence they saw no objection to bringing ideas within the mind, making them actually *part* of the mind, if not the whole of it.

But there is a deeper pressure operating, which not merely makes this move natural for an Empiricist but actually makes it inevitable, once a certain view of ideas is accepted. Berkeley argued that the very esse of ideas was percipi, that it involved a contradiction to say that ideas could exist unperceived. And even though it be a mistake to speak of the *perception* of ideas, we have agreed that he is essentially right. Against Russell, we argued that the concept of a sense-impression no-one was having was an incoherent one. (Clearly the same goes for sensations and mental images.) Yet, as we have just seen, Berkeley wanted to say at the same time that minds are quite distinct from their ideas. But the question then arises how there can be a necessary connection between two distinct things. There may be a contingent connection, it may be a fact that whenever one is found the other is also found, and vice-versa, but there can be no question of a logically necessary connection.[1] The point is the same as one of Hume's points about the relation of cause and effect. Since the cause is *one* event, and the effect *another* event, therefore, Hume argues, there can be no logically necessary connection between the two, but only a connection discovered by experience.

But if, nevertheless, we still insist that there *is* a logically necessary connection between 'ideas' and the mind that has them (and we have argued that Berkeley was right so to insist), then our conclusion can only be that the mind is *not* something distinct from its ideas, that they are actually the stuff of the mind. We need not say that ideas are the only things that go to make up the mind, it may include thoughts and emotions also, if these are something more than ideas. It may even include a simple indivisible soul-object. But ideas will have to be included.

[1] We shall not argue for, but will simply assume, this fundamental principle of Empiricism in the course of this book.

This is the real logical basis of Hume's 'bundle' theory of the mind, this is the reason for identifying the mind with the 'stream of consciousness'. Our sense-impressions are mind-dependent, they cannot exist except in relation to a mind. They are therefore part of the mind. The mind *is*, in part at least, a succession of sense-impressions.[1] (Exactly the same argument proves that our sensations, mental images, thoughts and emotions are also part of the mind, for they cannot exist without somebody having them.)

Sense-impressions, therefore, and all other 'items of consciousness', must be brought within the mind. They cannot be held at a distance from it, as Berkeley tried to hold them, for they have a necessary connection with the mind. But, as we shall now see, there are great difficulties in combining the views that: (i) our sense-impressions are part of our minds; (ii) physical objects are constructions out of sense-impressions. We shall examine three of the principal difficulties.

1. We normally think of the mind that perceives an object as one thing, and the object that is perceived as another thing distinct from the perceiver. Now, suppose we combine the Empiricist view that sense-impressions are part of the mind, with the Phenomenalist account of physical objects. We reach the conclusion that, since both minds and physical objects are constructions out of sense-impressions (even if, in the case of minds, sense-impressions are not the only sort of thing that go to make up a mind), there is what might be called an *overlap* between perceiver and perceived. For to perceive a physical object is to have a certain sense-impression which is a member of a certain collection of sense-impressions. But this sense-impression is also a constituent part of the collection of items that constitutes a mind, and the other members of the physical-object collection are constituents of other minds, or of the same mind at other times.

This partial identity between the mind that perceives and the thing that is perceived is a strange doctrine, and seems to constitute a serious criticism of Phenomenalism. Nevertheless, certain thinkers were prepared to swallow the paradox and to combine

[1] Cf. Berkeley 'Philosophical Commentaries', Entry 580: 'Mind is a congeries of Perceptions. Take away Perceptions and you take away the Mind, put the Perceptions and you put the mind'. (*Works* Vol. I, ed. A. A. Luce.)

Phenomenalism with the 'bundle' theory of the mind. We find such a doctrine in Ernst Mach[1] and in Bertrand Russell.[2] (Russell bases his position to some extent on William James and the American 'Neutral Monists' who were influenced by James.) On this view, to talk about minds, and to talk about physical objects, is to group the same sense-impressions in two different ways. A schematic diagram will make the situation clear. It represents three minds M_1, M_2, M_3 which, during a certain stretch of time, perceive in the same order the physical objects P_1, P_2, P_3.

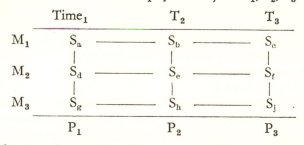

If the sense-impressions (S) are grouped horizontally we have the three minds between T_1 and T_3. If they are grouped vertically we have the physical object P_1 at T_1, the physical object P_2 at T_2, and the physical object P_3 at T_3. The materials out of which mind and matter are composed are exactly the same, that is, sense-impressions. It may be that the horizontal groupings will have to include other objects besides sense-impressions, for example, sensations, mental images, thoughts and emotions, but this will be the only major correction that needs to be made.

As I have said, the necessity for accepting such a world-picture seems a serious criticism of Phenomenalism. But since some Phenomenalists have been prepared to accept the picture, it cannot be considered a conclusive criticism.

2. But our discussion has uncovered a deeper problem for the Phenomenalist. What is it that makes us say that all our sense-impressions, and other items of consciousness, belong to one mind? What makes my sense-impressions today and my sense-impressions yesterday, part of the same mind?

Now, of course, this problem is not peculiar to Phenomenalism, for it is the problem of the nature of personal identity, or one facet of that problem. But the acceptance of Phenomenalism does rule

[1] Cf. *The Analysis of Sensations.*   [2] Cf. *The Analysis of Mind.*

out one particularly hopeful line of solution. For once we accept the analysis of physical objects in terms of sense-impressions, we cannot use the *body* to explain why certain sense-impressions, or other items of consciousness, are grouped together as belonging to one mind. This makes the problem peculiarly difficult for the Phenomenalist.

If we cannot make the body a uniting principle, then, why do we group together the items that make up a mind? The problem could be solved if our sense-impressions, and other experiences, could be taken to be mere predicates or qualifications of an underlying soul-substance. But such a solution would have to face most serious criticisms, and in any case is unlikely to appeal to the Phenomenalist. Among other difficulties, physical objects would become constructions out of the predicates of souls. Some other solution must be found.

I think this is the problem that Hume confesses himself defeated by in the Appendix to his *Treatise*. Hume recognises three associative principles which tend to make us mark off a collection of items by a single name, viz. similarity, contiguity and causation. Contiguity is clearly irrelevant here, because the different items that make up a mind are not spatially related. So attention must be restricted to similarity and causation. Now there is no doubt that there are resemblances between a man's present sense-impressions, sensations, mental images, thoughts and emotions, and those he had previously. There is no doubt, also, that his past experiences are one of the factors that causally determines the nature of his present experience. But do these relations of resemblance and causation really suffice to mark off *all* the experiences that I call *my* experiences from everybody else's experiences? It seems very doubtful. Other people's experiences may resemble mine or be causally determined by mine; while, on the other hand, I might have a quite novel experience that was in no way like, and in no way caused by, my past experiences.

The same sort of difficulty arises if we try to use *memory* to provide the uniting principle. It is true that a large part of our experience involves either memory of other parts of our experience, or is itself remembered at some other time. And so we may be able to construct a network of memory links which unites many of the experiences of the one person, and includes nothing outside his experiences. But the difficulty lies in extending this to *all* our

experiences. I remember seeing Chartres Cathedral. But there must
have been many features of the experience which are in no way
linked by memory to the rest of my experience, especially what
Leibniz would have called my 'petites perceptions' on this occasion. It is true that these forgotten experiences *accompanied* other
experiences that I do remember, but 'accompanying' here only
means 'part of my mind', and this is the very thing we are trying
to define. Nor does it seem sufficient to eke out the memory-
relationships by the relations of similarity and causation.

And so we find A. J. Ayer, for instance, writing:

> We have not succeeded in discovering any relation by which the
> constituents of Hume's bundles could be adequately held together.
> Some continuity of memory is necessary, but not, I think, suffi-
> cient. It needs to be backed by some other relation of which,
> perhaps, nothing more illuminating can be said than that it is the
> relation that holds between experiences when they are constituents
> of the same consciousness.[1]

At one time I thought that the Phenomenalist could only provide a uniting relation by this sort of *ad hoc* postulation. This
would be a serious criticism of his position. However, I have
since come to think that this is not true. And so, although I am
here putting forward *criticisms* of Phenomenalism, I will indicate
how the Phenomenalist can solve this problem about personal
identity.

We have seen earlier that the Phenomenalist must say that our
experience of time is derived from our perception of the succession
and co-existence of our *own* sense-impressions and other experiences. The temporal relations that hold between our experiences and other people's experiences are relations which he
has to treat, like all other features of the public world, as constructions out of everybody's private experiences. Now all our
experiences are experienced as linked to each other by temporal
relations, and our immediate experience of time is confined to our
own experiences. Here, then, is the uniting relation the Phenomenalist requires.

The experiences that constitute my mind, are all those, and only
those, amongst which I immediately perceive temporal relations.
Of course I do not perceive a temporal relation between *any* two of

[1] *The Problem of Knowledge*, pp. 225–6.

my experiences. But it seems quite plausible to say that, given any experience of mine, it will be linked by an immediately perceived relation of co-existence or succession to some other experience of mine, and that this other experience will be similarly linked to further experiences of mine, and so on indefinitely. In this way it might be possible to pass, step by step, from any experience of mine to any other experience, by means of immediately perceived temporal relations. And since, for the Phenomenalist, our immediate experience of time is confined to perception of our own sense-impressions and other experiences, the chain of experiences will never include any except mine.

It is true that we might think of some experiences that were difficult to deal with in this way. Consider, for instance, a dream that involved no thought of my past, and that was not remembered after waking. There would be no possible perception of temporal links between it and my other experiences. But perhaps the account of the unity of the mind in terms of immediately perceived temporal relations could be supplemented by bringing in further relations to deal with such difficult cases. It might even be possible to appeal to the body as a uniting principle, provided we went on to give an account of the body in terms of sense-impressions.

So perhaps the Phenomenalist can solve Hume's problem. But, as we have seen, he can do it only by insisting on the subjectivity of our experience of time. In doing so, he is providing the starting-point for our fourth argument against Phenomenalism; that is, our argument that the Phenomenalist can give no satisfactory account of public time.

3. But now we pass on to another criticism of the 'bundle' theory of the mind which seems to involve insuperable problems for the Phenomenalist. If we talk about a bundle or collection of twigs, this implies that the individual twigs are things that exist in their own right, independently of the bundle. They are in the bundle, but it is perfectly conceivable that they should not be in the bundle, we can conceive of their existing outside the bundle. It is the same with the soldiers that make up an army. It is true that this case is a little different, because we should not call them 'soldiers' unless they occur in the bundle of persons that constitutes the army, but we could still conceive of their existing outside the bundle under another description.

Now if we are going to take *seriously* the notion that the mind is a 'bundle of experiences', then it seems we shall have to make the same admission in this case also. But can we admit that the items that make up our 'stream of consciousness' are capable of an independent existence outside that stream? Consider the case of sense-impressions. The 'bundle' theory says that for a mind to have a sense-impression is for that sense-impression to be a member of a certain collection of experiences. But if this sense-impression could exist outside the collection, we would have a sense-impression that *nobody is having*. But this, we decided previously, is a nonsensical conception. Hence this argument provides a *reductio ad absurdum* of the 'bundle' theory of the mind.

The Phenomenalist can have no hope of meeting this argument by treating our experiences as mere predicates or qualifications of our bodies, and so making them something that could not have independent existence. For as we have pointed out *ad nauseam*, in his view bodies themselves are collections of sense-impressions. Such a line of escape is open to a Realist, but not to a Phenomenalist.

It is true that the Phenomenalist could treat our experiences as predicates or qualifications of a soul-substance. But such a view is hardly likely to appeal to him. It will be time enough to argue against it when it is adopted. In default of such a view, the Phenomenalist must take sense-impressions to be particulars or substances out of which the mind is constructed.

In the *Problem of Knowledge* Ayer recognizes the serious difficulty for Phenomenalism here and proposes the following way out.[1] He agrees that it is not logically necessary for any particular experience to belong to any particular group of items that constitute a mind. It is logically possible that the sense-impressions I am having now should not be part of my experience, but should instead be part of yours. But, Ayer suggests, it is nevertheless logically necessary that any experience belong to *some* large bundle of experiences, that is, that it be part of *some* mind. In this way Ayer hopes to escape the difficulties involved in saying that it is possible for there to be sense-impressions nobody is having, without completely abandoning the view that the self is a bundle of distinct experiences. His position is very like those who argue

[1] Chap. 5, sec. (ii), pp. 223–6.

against Hume that, although it is a contingent matter what *sort* of cause brings about a particular effect, it is nevertheless logically necessary that every event have *some* cause.

Ayer's compromise seems to be an unacceptable one. Consider the parallel situation with regard to cause and effect. The reason for denying that there can be any logically necessary connection between cause and effect is that they are *two distinct events*, and that the existence of one event cannot entail the existence of another. But if this is so, it seems that we must also deny that it is logically necessary that every event have a cause. For if an event entails the existence of some cause, it entails the existence of a distinct event. It is irrelevant that nothing is entailed about the *nature* of that distinct event. In just the same way, to say that minds are bundles of items, items which can never occur outside such bundles, is to imply that the existence of an event (e.g. the occurrence of a certain sense-impression) entails the existence of other events (the other items of the bundle), even although it does not entail that the other events be of a certain definite nature.

A subsidiary difficulty here is the question how large the 'bundle' will have to be before we count it as a bundle. My momentary sense-impression is clearly not capable of independent existence. Would two such experiences be in any better position? Or three? The arbitrariness of any particular limitation that we place on the minimum size of bundles indicates the unstable nature of Ayer's compromise.

So it appears that the only way left to the Phenomenalist is to argue that there is nothing impossible about an item of consciousness, such as a sense-impression, existing independently of any consciousness. He must defend the possibility of unsensed sense-impressions, unsensed sensibilia. But this possibility we have already considered and rejected. In chapter IV we based our rejection of this possibility on the fact that the term 'sense-impression' is introduced by reference to the way things appear *to people*, and cannot be detached from this. An additional argument may be drawn from our conclusion that at least some sense-impressions are indeterminate in character. An indeterminate sense-impression seems to be quite clearly an abstraction from a wider situation—that of a *person* who has certain indeterminate impressions. It seems peculiarly repugnant to conceive of a sense-impression all or some of whose characteristics are indeterminate, but which nevertheless lives a life of splendid isolation from any consciousness. Yet, if the 'bundle' theory of mind be correct, then it seems that this must be possible.

Phenomenalism thus suffers a final shipwreck on the problem of the nature of the mind.

7

AN ANALYSIS OF SENSORY ILLUSION[1]

Our examination of the Representative and the Phenomenalist theories could be said to have been a digression from the main line of the argument. We had been examining the Argument from Illusion, which seemed to show that, whether we are perceiving a physical object as it really is, or whether we are suffering from sensory illusion, the immediate object of apprehension is always a sense-impression or sense-datum. We might then have gone on to consider whether an account of sensory illusion could be given which would evade the conclusion that the Argument from Illusion seeks to draw. But then it might have been asked 'Why *ought* we to evade the conclusion of the Argument from Illusion?' So, in order to convince ourselves that we must seek an alternative account of sensory illusion, we tried *accepting* the argument, and then seeing where it led us. We saw that, if the immediate object of apprehension in perception is a sense-impression, then we must go on to accept some version of the Representative or the Phenomenalist account of perception. But an examination of both these theories revealed fatal difficulties. So now we have been sufficiently emboldened to go back and re-examine the Argument from Illusion.

[1] Some of what I say in this chapter I have anticipated in the article 'Illusions of Sense' mentioned in chap. 1.

AN ANALYSIS OF SENSORY ILLUSION

Any account of sensory illusion must fulfil two demands. (i) It must account for the *likeness* between sensory illusion and veridical perception, the likeness between 'seeing' snakes that are not there, and seeing actual snakes, or the likeness between 'seeing' that the stick in water is bent, and seeing as bent a stick that is actually bent. That is to say, it must be able to explain why it is that what is in fact a veridical perception might have been an illusory perception, and vice versa. The supporters of the Argument from Illusion want to say that the likeness springs from the likenesses of the sense-impressions which are the immediate objects of apprehension in both cases. (ii) But there is a difference between sensory illusion and veridical perception, and the second demand that any analysis of sensory illusion must fulfil is to give an account of this difference which will yet be compatible with an admission of the similarities holding between the two. The supporters of the Argument from Illusion divide here. Upholders of the Representative theory say that, in the case of veridical perception, the sense-impression which is the immediate object of apprehension is a correct picture or representation of a physical reality that is *not* immediately perceivable. In sensory illusion there is a more or less radical failure of the sense-impression to picture or to represent physical reality. Phenomenalists, on the other hand, say that, in the case of veridical perception, the sense-impression which is the immediate object of apprehension *coheres with*, or *fits in with*, the other sense-impressions that we or other people have. In sensory illusion there is a more or less radical lack of such coherence with the rest of immediate experience.

The question now arises whether we can give some alternative account of sensory illusion which will also do justice to its resemblances to, and differences from, veridical perception, but will avoid the fatal difficulties which beset the two accounts we have already discussed.

We may start by remembering that there is a connection between sensory illusion and *false belief*, as indeed the word 'illusion' makes clear. If I go into a room and have an hallucinatory visual experience as of a cat on the mat, then, under normal circumstances, I shall have a false belief about the world, viz. that there is a cat on the mat now. This suggests a first attempt to solve our problem. Let us try saying that to undergo sensory illusion is simply to hold a false belief about our environment: to think that something exists in it, or that something has a certain property, when this is not so. And, in order to keep the parallel between sensory illusion and veridical perception, we shall have to say that the latter is just a matter of holding true beliefs about our environment.

If this answer were correct, we would be rid of the problems that arise when we say that in sensory illusion there is an existent, although non-physical, object which is the immediate object of perception, viz. a sense-impression. Suppose I believe that the centre of the earth is inhabited, and that my belief is false. I do not stand in any relation to a quasi-object or a quasi-state of affairs 'the inhabited centre of the earth' or 'the fact that the centre of the earth is inhabited'. For, *pace* Meinong, there is no such object or state of affairs, and so I cannot have any relation to it. And if sensory illusion is simply a false belief about the world around us, we do not need to postulate an object, the sense-impression, to which we have a relation when we suffer sensory illusion.

Now in a later chapter we hope to show just how much merit this suggestion has. But here our concern must be to see that the reduction will not do as it stands. Consider two situations: (i) I come into a room and have an hallucinatory experience as of a cat on the mat; (ii) I do not go into the room, but somebody whom I trust tells me what is not true, viz. that there is a cat on the mat. Now in both cases I would normally have a false belief. And in the second case, it may well be, all that I would have is a false belief. But in the first case it seems there is very much more to the matter. In some sense of the word, am I not *seeing*? Is there not a black cat-like shape *in my visual field*, even if there is no such thing in physical reality? And does this not show that sensory illusion is not merely false belief? And now it may seem that we ought to say that in sensory illusion we have a false belief *based on* an immediate apprehension or perception of a non-physical object, the sense-impression.

Now it is true that there is a difference between sensory illusion and mere false belief that something is the case in our environment. But is the difference anything more than an *additional* false belief? Let us now try saying that, when we have an hallucination as of a cat on the mat, we not only acquire a false belief about the physical world (viz. that there is a cat on the mat), but we also acquire the belief *that we are now seeing*[1] *the cat*. After all, if I do have such an hallucination I will (normally) believe two things: (i) there is a cat on the mat before me; (ii) I am seeing that cat. The suggestion being put forward now is only that the occurrence of these two false beliefs *constitutes* sensory illusion, that this is all that sensory illusion *is*. In sensory illusion there is no 'perception' of a quasi-object, but simply a false belief that there is ordinary veridical perception of an ordinary physical object or state of affairs.

What about the parallel that we must retain between sensory illusion and veridical perception, the parallel on which the Argument from Illusion rightly insists, even if it goes on to use it to draw the wrong conclusions? Well, suppose I come into a room, and really do see a cat on the mat. Normally, I shall believe that I am *seeing* the cat. (This is shown by the fact that if I am asked how I know the cat is there I can reply 'I can *see* it'.) So a veridical perception normally involves exactly the same two beliefs as the corresponding sensory illusion, which gives us the parallel we require. The difference is given by the fact that in the case of veridical perception the beliefs are true, in the case of sensory illusion the beliefs are false.

All the same, it will be replied, when we are subject to sensory illusion, as in the case of the cat, there is an object in my visual field which no attempted analysis of sensory illusion in terms of false belief can possibly conjure away. My false beliefs that there is a cat on the mat, and that I am seeing the cat, are *based* on an immediate acquaintance with this (non-physical) object. To say otherwise is to try to talk away something that is visibly there.

This objection is very natural, but completely mistaken. However it does enable us to make quite clear the nature of the analysis of sensory illusion that we are offering. What we are asserting is just what this objection says it is incredible to assert, viz. that when (or in so far as) we suffer from sensory illusion there is no object at all, physical or non-physical, which we are perceiving in any possible sense of the word 'perceiving'. There is simply the (completely) false belief that ordinary perceiving is taking place. We can, if we wish, talk about there being an 'object

[1] Notice that the word 'see' is used here in its normal sense, the sense which implies the physical existence of the thing seen.

in our visual field' or about our 'having a sense-impression'. These phrases have their uses. But we must remember that they are systematically misleading in a philosophical context. They can be replaced without remainder by statements that we falsely believe that we are perceiving something.

But if this is all there is to sensory illusion why do we *seem to ourselves* to be perceiving something? But is the situation any different from any other case of false belief? If I (sincerely) believe that the moon is made of green cheese, it must *seem to me* that the moon is made of green cheese. If it did not, I could not be said to believe this about the moon. So if I (*sincerely*) believe that I am now seeing a cat (although there is no cat there), must it not *seem to me* just as if I am seeing a cat? If it does not seem this way to me, I would not believe I am seeing a cat. The non-physical object of immediate apprehension is simply a ghost generated by my belief that I am seeing something. We recognise that in cases where we are hallucinated our belief is false, so we do not say that there is a *physical* object or state of affairs corresponding to the belief. But, perhaps because we trust the senses so deeply, we still cannot bring ourselves to admit that the belief is wholly false. So we postulate a compromise object, the sense-impression, and say that we *do* 'see' it. Ultimately the error is the same as Meinong's errors about the object of thought and belief. So far, then, it seems quite satisfactory to say that to be under sensory illusion is to have the false belief that we are perceiving some physical existent.

2. 'PERCEPTION WITHOUT BELIEF'

But at this point we must come to terms with a much more serious objection, which threatens to wreck our whole analysis of sensory illusion. Despite the word 'illusion', it may be pointed out, sensory illusion can occur without any false belief at all. Suppose I am regularly subject to hallucinations, such as those of seeming to see cats, under certain conditions which I know and can recognise. Under these circumstances, I may well come to recognise my hallucination for what it is, an hallucination. I will not believe that there is a cat on the mat, and, *a fortiori*, I will not believe that I am seeing a cat. Yet there certainly is a black cat-like shape 'in my visual field'. A more familiar example is provided by mirrors. Every day I look into a mirror to comb my hair or to shave. The visual appearance I am presented with is that of a being like myself *behind* the physical surface of the mirror, where there is no such actual object. Now when I first looked into a mirror as a child it may well have deceived me. I may have thought I was looking at another child. Even now, if I do not know that it is a mirror I am looking at, I may be momentarily deceived into thinking that I am looking at another person. But normally the irregular visual appearance involves no such false belief. It seems to follow that our analysis of sensory illusion has left something out. It seems that the false belief that I am perceiving something is generated by something else, the sense-impression which I have, which is the *immediate* object of perception.

The point that has just been developed is fairly familiar. But it is not so often noticed that the same sort of thing can happen in veridical perception. Suppose that there is a cat on the mat, and that I see it. But suppose I have been having a lot of hallucinations of cats recently, so that I have become suspicious. I may 'discount appearances' and decide there is no cat there, although there really is. Here I certainly perceive the cat, but I do not believe the cat is there, nor do I believe that I am seeing it. Once again, it seems that this can only be explained by saying there is a 'visual appearance' involved which is the immediate object of perception, and on which my beliefs, if any, are founded.

These cases where we disbelieve our perceptions ('perception without belief' we will call them) constitute a serious difficulty for our analysis of sensory illusion. But we shall find that we need only amend the analysis, not abandon it altogether. The first point to be made is that 'perception without belief' only occurs where we have independent information that runs counter to the 'evidence of the senses'. The man who has hallucinations of cats, but treats the hallucinations for what they are, can do this only because past experience has assured him that there can be no cat there. In default of this independent information he would 'believe his eyes'. When we look at a mirror we escape deception only because of a long familiarity with mirrors and their tricky ways. If we are ignorant of mirrors, or if we do not know that it is a *mirror* that is in front of us, we will be deceived by appearances. This point holds however unusual the sensory phenomena may be. But for what I know of the world, when I have spots before my eyes I should think there are coloured objects floating before me (it is said that babies actually try to brush them away). If my visual impressions blur because my eyes fill with tears, it is only what I know of the world that enables me to realise that the physical objects before me are not dissolving or wavering. The 'duplication' of the world that occurs when I press my eye-ball I should take to be a real duplication, but for my independent knowledge that this is not so.

In all cases of 'perception without belief,' therefore, there would be belief that we are perceiving something, but for independently acquired information. Formally, we have a contrary-to-fact conditional statement 'If I did not know or believe X, then I would believe I was perceiving a Y'.[1] Whenever 'perception without belief' occurs, such a statement will be true.

The question then arises what sort of contrary-to-fact conditional statements we are dealing with here. Are they like 'If you had been bitten by that spider, you would have been very sick'? This statement is *empirically* true. It is empirically true that the bite of spiders of that sort is dangerous, and so the contrary-to-fact statement is also empirically true. Or are they like 'If he had been a father, he would have been a male parent'? This second statement is logically necessary. Now it seems to me that the contrary-to-fact conditional statements that we are dealing with here are logically necessary statements. If I have an hallucination of a cat, and if I have no independent information of any sort which suggests that I am not looking at a cat, then it is logically necessary that I will believe that I am looking at a cat. If I perceive an actual cat (perceiving it *as* a cat), and if there is nothing to suggest I am being hallucinated, then it is logically necessary that I will believe I am looking at a cat. 'Perception without belief', then, is *essentially belief-inducing*; in default of other, contradictory, beliefs it must issue in the belief that we are perceiving something in our environment.

How shall we characterise 'perception without belief' then? If I am correct in saying that it is *essentially* belief-inducing, then it seems to follow that it must involve the *thought* that we are perceiving something in the world, a thought held back from being a belief by other, contradictory, beliefs. As we may put it, it is a

[1] Notice that contrary-to-fact conditional statements of this sort are not confined to the field of perception. Consider e.g. 'If I did not know you so well, I would have thought you were joking.'

thought that *presses towards* being a belief. Such a thought I shall describe as an 'inclination to believe'. I am not very happy about this phrase 'inclination to believe', for it could have misleading implications. But I cannot find a better phrase, and so beg leave to use it as a technical term in the rest of this book.

We may now re-formulate our analysis of sensory illusion. We shall say that sensory illusion is nothing but false belief, *or inclination to a false belief*, that we are perceiving some physical object or state of affairs. And the parallel with veridical perception can be maintained because, when we really perceive, we will normally believe we are perceiving, or, where this belief is lacking, there will be an inclination to believe we are perceiving. There has been no need to postulate a special object to be the immediate object of perception in sensory illusion. Where we have an hallucination as of a cat before us, there is no object at all to be perceived. We only think or are inclined to think that we perceive such an object. When the stick put in water looks bent, there is nothing bent to be perceived, we only think or are inclined to think we perceive such an object. We may talk about 'sense-impressions' or even about 'objects in our sensory field' but we must not be led into postulating substances to correspond to these substantive phrases. 'To have a sense-impression which does not correspond to reality' is only to think, or be inclined to think, we perceive, when in fact we do not perceive.

3. IS 'PERCEPTION WITHOUT BELIEF' ESSENTIALLY BELIEF-INDUCING?

But before going on, let us look more carefully at our contention (central to our argument) that 'perception without belief' is essentially belief-inducing. It may be agreed that 'perception without belief' only occurs where we have other beliefs about our environment which lead us to deny the judgement we would naturally come to on the basis of our perceptual experience. But, it may be maintained, this is a mere contingent fact. We could conceive of ourselves having exactly the same perceptual experience that we have when we think we are seeing a cat; we could conceive, furthermore, that we had no reason to deny that there was a physical cat there; and yet, it will be argued, we could conceive of ourselves having no belief or inclination to believe that we were seeing a cat. This implies that there are *two* elements involved in sensory illusion: (i) the belief or inclination to believe that we are perceiving a certain physical object or state of affairs; (ii) the perceptual experience or sense-impression on which this belief is founded.

(1) One argument may be offered in support of this view which deserves attention. Suppose I have the hallucination as of hearing a car outside. I falsely believe, or am inclined to believe, that I hear a car. But might not somebody who knew nothing of cars have exactly the same perceptual experience? Yet he would only believe, or be inclined to believe, that he was hearing a certain sort of noise. Here the sense-impressions are the same, but the false belief, or inclination to believe, is different. So it seems we ought to distinguish our sense-impressions from our beliefs or inclinations to believe that we are perceiving something.

However, this objection does not refute our analysis, although it does draw attention to a point so far overlooked. Here we must recall the distinction we drew in Chapter 2, where we said that the noise of a coach outside was *immediately* heard, while the coach itself was only *mediately* perceived, through experience of the particular noise coaches make. (In speaking of the noise of the coach here, we mean the happening in the objective world, we do not mean that it is our sense-impression of the noise of the coach which is immediately perceived. To say the latter is the error of the Argument from Illusion.) We can now use the distinction between immediate and mediate perception to refine our account of what it is to have a sense-impression. We said before that to have a sense-impression is to believe, or be inclined to believe, that we are perceiving something. We now say that to have a sense-impression is to believe, or to be inclined to believe, that we are *immediately* perceiving something. Thus, if somebody has an hallucination of a cat, his false belief about what he is *immediately* seeing will not be that he sees a cat, but that he sees a thing of a certain colour and shape. And *this* is what we call 'his sense-impression' or 'the object in his visual field'. As we saw in the case of the car, different people could have different beliefs about what they were *mediately* perceiving, although holding the same beliefs about what they were *immediately* perceiving. But this does nothing to refute our identification of sense-impressions with beliefs, or inclinations to believe, that we are perceiving something.

88

We need only add that they are beliefs or inclinations to believe that something is *immediately* perceived.

(2) Even so, it will still be argued, there is a distinction between sense-impressions, on the one hand, and belief or inclination to believe that we are immediately perceiving something, on the other. The two may in fact always be found together, but it is logically possible, at least, to have the first without the second. We shall therefore propose an argument to show that there can be no such distinction.

Now, if this view were taken, what would be the relationship between the sense-impression and the belief or inclination to believe we are immediately[1] perceiving some physical state of affairs? Does having a certain sense-impression *entail* having a certain belief or inclination to believe? If it does, then 'having a sense-impression' already involves having a certain belief or inclination to believe, and so the sense-impression is not distinct from the belief or inclination to believe, which is contrary to the hypothesis.[2]

The alternatives to this seem to be: (*a*) the sense-impression is a mere mental accompaniment of the belief or inclination to believe we are perceiving some state of affairs; (*b*) the sense-impression is the accompaniment and cause of the belief or inclination to believe we are perceiving some state of affairs; (*c*) the sense-impression is the accompaniment, cause and finally the *basis* or *ground* of our belief or inclination to believe we are perceiving some state of affairs.

Now, if positions (*a*) or (*b*) are adopted, I do not see how they are to be refuted. (At the same time I do not believe that there are such accompaniments or causes of our beliefs or inclinations to believe we are perceiving.) But if either position is true, the role of sense-impressions in perception is not logically important. We could pay such sense-impressions our phenomenological respects, and pass them by. But I take it that, in the original objection,

---

[1] Strictly speaking, once we admit the notion of sense-impressions on which our immediate perceptions are based, we shall no longer call them *immediate* perceptions. But it will be convenient, and I hope not misleading, to ignore this point in the course of this section.

[2] This would not be true if there were an *a priori* but synthetic connection between sense-impressions and beliefs or inclinations to believe. Here I can only say dogmatically that, as an Empiricist, I reject the possibility of synthetic *a priori* connection.

sense-impressions are thought of as the *basis* or *ground* or *evidence* for our beliefs or inclinations to believe we are perceiving. The question must therefore arise how these sense-impressions can act as such a basis, ground or evidence. As we have seen, they cannot entail the belief or inclination to believe. It seems, therefore, that the only way that such sense-impressions could underpin the beliefs or inclinations to believe would be by our having previously discovered a contingent connection that generally held between having the sense-impression and perceiving a certain state of affairs. But in order to discover this contingent connection, we would first have to have some way of discovering the nature of physical reality independently of our having sense-impressions.

It would seem, then, that we were faced with the problem of breaking out beyond our sense-impressions to physical reality. In other words, we are faced with the problems of the Representative theory of perception, which we have already declared to be insuperable. The only alternative would be to reduce physical reality to sense-impressions: to give an account of physical reality solely in terms of sense-impressions which cohere with each other in a certain way. But this is to accept Phenomenalism and its insuperable problems. So it seems that if we distinguish between sense-impressions, on the one hand, and our beliefs or inclinations to believe we are perceiving some state of affairs, on the other, and yet we make sense-impressions the ground or basis of the latter, we are led to untenable positions, viz. Representationalism or Phenomenalism.

There is another line of attack on this attempt to distinguish sense-impressions from beliefs or inclinations to believe we are (immediately) perceiving something, which may in the end come to the same thing. If there is only a contingent connection between the having of a sense-impression and the belief or inclination to believe we are (immediately) perceiving something, then it ought to be possible to characterise the sense-impression in other ways than by appealing to the belief (inclination to believe). Thus, there is a contingent connection between father and son, for the father is the cause, or at any rate a part cause, of the existence of the latter. But the characterisation 'father' is not logically independent of the causal relation a father has to a son. However it is possible to characterise the being that begets a son in a way that is independent of this causal relationship e.g. as a man. Now it may well be that, on any showing, the most *convenient* way of characterising our sense-impressions or perceptual experiences would be to say 'It is the sort of experience that makes me believe, or inclines me to believe, that I am perceiving an object of a certain sort'. But if there is only a contingent connection between sense-impressions and beliefs or inclinations to believe, it must be possible to give the former an independent characterisation, however inconvenient it may be for us, or however little interested we may be in doing so.

But is such independent characterisation in fact possible? Sense-impressions are 'private' objects so we cannot *point* to them as we point to physical objects. We might try speaking of 'the experience I am having now', but the difficulty then is that we have to distinguish the 'sense-impression experience' from any other experience we may happen to have at the same time.

Well then, what about our ordinary descriptive vocabulary? Perhaps we can say that there is a red, oval object in my visual field, or a loud bang in my auditory field, or a certain smell in my olfactory field. Here, however, we have to remember that such words as 'red', 'oval', 'loud', 'smelly', are learnt by reference to objects or events in the physical world, and can only be so learnt. We apply the words in the first place to red oval objects or to noisy and smelly places. So the question arises whether these words retain their ordinary sense when we use them to describe sense-impressions. Now in fact there is a clear difference of sense. This is shown by the fact that the things we can say about red balls, on the one hand, and red patches in the visual field, on the other, are quite different. For instance, it is possible to be mistaken about whether the ball is red, but it is not possible to be mistaken in thinking a certain portion of the visual field is red. So the question arises what it means to say that a certain sense-impression is red. What sort of characterisation is it that we are applying?

I think the only way to explain the meaning of descriptive words when applied to sense-impressions is to appeal to certain perceptual verbs. When it *looks* red to me now, *sounds* loud to me now, *tastes* sour to me now, then we can say I have a red visual impression, a loud auditory impression, a sour gustatory impression. In the statement 'It looks red to me now' the word 'red' has its ordinary physical-object meaning, 'red' means red as the

Red Flag is red. In the statement 'It sounds loud to me now' the word 'loud' means loud as an explosion is loud. But the addition of the verbs 'looks' and 'sounds' gives us phrases which enable us to say what we mean by 'red' and 'loud' as applied to sense-impressions. To have a red sense-impression means to have the sense-impression I have when something *looks* (physically) red to me now.

Now I think that there is no doubt that these phrases *do* enable us to describe our sense-impressions. If we use these perceptual verbs in their perceptual sense (as opposed to such metaphorical uses as 'This argument *looks* correct to me') they can be used to report on the nature of our sense-impressions. But we have been arguing that 'to have a sense-impression' is nothing distinct from believing or being inclined to believe that we are (immediately) perceiving objects or states of affairs of a certain sort. And the question now arises whether 'It looks red to me now', 'It tastes sour to me now', are not simply other ways of expressing our belief or inclination to believe that we are perceiving something? For, as has been pointed out by a number of recent writers, the language of 'looks', 'sounds', 'smells', 'feels', etc., is the normal vehicle for *tentative perception-claims*, tentative claims to perceive things of a certain sort. To say 'It looks oval to me' usually means that I have some inclination to believe that I am seeing something oval. So at this point it seems that the attempt to give sense-impressions a characterisation independent of beliefs or inclinations to believe we are perceiving something has failed.

But perhaps an opponent will not be daunted even by this. Perhaps he will claim boldly that words like 'looks', 'feels', 'sounds', etc., are used *in two different ways.* He will have to admit that there is a use in which such words make tentative perception-claims. But he will argue that there is a second sense of the statement 'It looks red to me now' where there is reference only to the perceptual experiences on which these beliefs are based. 'It looks red to me now' may either make a tentative claim, or it may simply register the having of a certain perceptual experience or sense-impression. The two things are not to be identified.[1]

Faced with this reply, I must confess I do not know how to argue any further. All one can do is to go back to the original objection to this separation of sense-impression and belief or in-

[1] Cf. Ayer *The Problem of Knowledge*, p. 112.

clination to believe we are perceiving something, and point out that such a position must lead either to a Representative or a Phenomenalist theory, theories which can be refuted on independent grounds. But in any case it seems simpler and more straight-forward to make no distinction between the having of a sense-impression and the believing or being inclined to believe we are (immediately) perceiving something.

4. A PSYCHOLOGICAL EXPLANATION OF THE OCCURRENCE OF SOME SENSORY ILLUSIONS

There is one final objection that might be brought against our analysis of sensory illusion. If, when we suffer sensory illusion, it is a mere matter of falsely believing or being inclined to believe that we are perceiving something, *why* do we come to hold these particular false beliefs or inclinations to believe? Why does the hallucinated man believe (or be inclined to believe) that he is seeing a cat? Why does the man who turns his eyes towards a mirror believe (or be inclined to believe) that he is seeing a mirror-double behind the surface of the glass? The theory that makes sense-impressions something distinct from beliefs or inclinations to believe we are perceiving at least provides an answer to this question. We come to these beliefs or inclinations to believe, the theory says, on the basis of sense-impressions, they supply the basis for the beliefs.

Now Hume has warned us against the intemperate search for causes, and we should equally restrain ourselves from an intemperate search for grounds for our beliefs. The grounds on which I accept a belief must be other things which I believe, and so, on pain of an infinite regress, I cannot find good reasons for *all* my beliefs. So why should not my false belief or inclination to believe that I am immediately perceiving something be one of those beliefs I just *find* myself with, without having any grounds for it?

I am suggesting, that is, that in the case of sensory illusion the appropriate thing is to look not for grounds for our beliefs, but only for causes. And this investigation into causes will not be a philosophical one, but rather a psychological, physiological or physical one. But although the matter is strictly outside our province, I want to put forward a psychological hypothesis which

93

I think does help to show how certain rather puzzling illusions arise.

Mirror-images, for instance, are one of these specially puzzling types of illusion. To a superficial investigation they might not seem to be illusory phenomena at all. For they are in some sense 'public' objects. Two people can see exactly the same mirror-image of a certain scene, although they may have to take it in turns to look in the mirror. Given a description of the mirror, the position and description of the objects imaged, and the position of the observer, the nature of the image can be worked out mathematically. All this may tempt us to treat mirror-images as physical objects, or at any rate entitled to rank among physical existents, even if *ultimus inter pares*. Mirror-images can even be photographed. This seems to show that they exist independently of being perceived; and that even when I am out of the room the mirror on the wall keeps on reflecting the furniture, and that in no mere hypothetical sense, but in the same sense that the wall retains its colour, size and shape when not perceived.

Now we have seen that it is in fact wrong to treat mirror-images as physical existents. For as we have remarked a number of times the image looks to be behind the physical surface of the glass, and it may well be that it is quite impossible for anything having the qualities of the image to exist in that place. (Suppose e.g. the mirror is on a thick wall.)[1] So we are definitely under the necessity of treating mirror-images as a species of sensory illusion. And if our analysis of sensory illusion is correct, this means that when we look at a mirror we believe falsely or are inclined to believe falsely that we see an object much like ourselves behind the surface of the glass. We are committed to saying that no substance (even a junior substance) corresponds to the substantive expression 'mirror-image'. Nevertheless, because of the characteristics of mirror-images mentioned in the previous paragraph, this analysis may not seem very plausible. So a psychological explanation of just how we come to be subject to this illusion would be very helpful to our argument.

But before tackling a difficult case like that of the mirror-image, let us work up to it by considering a much easier case where I believe the same psychological mechanism to be operating. Suppose

---

[1] Nor can we distinguish between the real and the apparent location of the image. The image is where it appears to be—that is, it is a sense-impression.

one crosses two adjoining fingers and then one puts a small ball or a pencil between them. It will feel as though we are touching not just one object, but two. How does this illusion occur? The explanation is that the sides of the fingers that are touching the object would not normally be next to each other, but would each be on the far side of the other. This means that *in normal circumstances*, that is, when our fingers are not crossed, if there were objects that were touching these two sides of the fingers, they would have to be *two different objects*. Now it is important to observe that when we put objects between adjoining fingers in normal circumstances, we do not merely perceive the object touched. We also have some awareness[1] of the fingers that are doing the touching, where they are in relation to the object touched, and to each other. Now I suggest that the illusion occurs because, even in the abnormal situation where the fingers are crossed, we have an inclination, which we cannot fully check, to assume that the objects doing the touching, that is, the fingers, *are situated normally*. (What we have is association by resemblance. We cannot help assuming that all cases will resemble the normal cases.) So even in cases where the fingers are crossed, we believe, or have an inclination to believe, that they are uncrossed. But, if the fingers were uncrossed, it is certain we would be touching not one object, but two. Hence we cannot help believing, or being inclined to believe, that we are touching two objects.

The general formula which we can derive from this simple case is that, when we perceive, we are regularly aware not only of the perceived object, but also of the conditions under which we are perceiving the object; we are aware of the relation of our own body and senses to the object perceived. The perception of the object, and the perception of the normal conditions under which it is perceived, become associated with each other. We then perceive the object in circumstances where the relation of our body and senses to the object perceived is *not* normal. But we still cannot help thinking or being inclined to think that the conditions of perception *are* normal, so we construe *what is perceived* to fit in with this wrong view that perceiving conditions are normal. If this account of the 'crossed fingers illusion' is correct, it would follow that if we always touched objects under the abnormal conditions, so that they eventually became thought of as normal, then the illusion

[1] But see the note to the next paragraph.

should vanish. Whether this is in fact so would have to be decided experimentally.[1]

Now let us apply the same methods to the case of the mirror-image. The first point to realize is that, when we look into a mirror, there is a sense in which what we see is *ourselves*. (We actually speak of seeing ourselves in the mirror.) But of course this is not the whole story, or else there would be no element of *illusion* involved. So the next point to realize is that we see ourselves *subject to certain distortions*. There is, firstly, distortion of place, for we see ourselves as being as far behind the surface of the glass as we are actually in front of it. Secondly, there is the characteristic left-right distortion. Nevertheless, we are seeing ourselves. However, and this is the vital point, we are seeing ourselves under highly unusual conditions, because the object we are looking at (ourselves), is not, as objects seen usually are, in front of our face. When we turn our eyes towards a mirror, we see in the first place the space between ourselves and the mirror. If the mirror were an opaque object we would see no further. If it were transparent we would see beyond it. But, as it is a mirror, we get something very curious, a view of the space between the mirror and ourselves *seen from the mirror end*. Our vision ranges across from ourselves to the mirror, and from the mirror back to ourselves. Now *normally* any object that we see is in front of our face, and moreover, this fact is something of which we are aware.[2] (We do not see our eyes,

[1] Professor J. J. C. Smart has pointed out to me that it may not even be necessary for us to be *aware* that conditions of perception are normal. Suppose, in the case we have been discussing, that physical stimulation of different portions of the fingers affects the *brain* in a different way, without our being aware of it. An 'association' might be built up in the brain between a certain sort of stimulation of certain parts of the fingers, and perception of the things normally perceived under those conditions of perception. When these parts of the fingers were stimulated in the same way under *abnormal* conditions (e.g. with our fingers crossed), the brain-mechanism might cause us to have a belief or inclination to believe that we were perceiving what we should *normally* perceive when these parts were stimulated in that way.

It would seem to be possible to decide experimentally whether *awareness* of the conditions of perception was essential or not in the causation of such sensory illusions.

[2] If Smart's suggestion is correct there will be no need for us to be *aware* of the relations of our body to the object perceived. It will simply be a matter of an 'association' in the *brain* between (i) perceiving a certain situation and (ii) having the eyes stimulated by light-waves entering the eye in the way that they *normally* do when that situation is perceived.

but we have marginal vision of our own face and some appreciation of its spatial relations to the object on which our eyes are
focused.) I suggest that in the case where we look at a mirror we
tend to think that all of what we are seeing is in front of our eyes,
and that we are having a perfectly normal view of it. Now, as mentioned, what we are seeing is, firstly, the space between ourselves
and the mirror, and, secondly, the space from the mirror to ourselves. We are simultaneously getting two views of the same area,
each from a different point of view. But we cannot accept the
second view as it stands, because here the relations of the object
seen to the organs of vision are not normal. So we tend to think
that what the second view gives us is simply an *extension* of the first
view: that we are seeing something that is in front of our eyes, and
beyond the object given us by the first view. But since in fact we are
really seeing the same area all over again from a different perspective, our face appears to be just as far behind the surface of the
glass as it is in fact in front of it. The left-hand side of the face
naturally seems to be behind the left-hand side of the mirror, and
the same holds for the centre and right-hand side. And since the
face we are seeing seems to be *facing* us (as objects that we see
normally are), we get the left–right distortion that mirrors give us.
Hence the image is not an exact copy of the object imaged, except
in the way that a left-hand glove copies a right-hand glove.

The 'public' character of mirror-images is thus explained, while
still maintaining that they are illusions or distortions of vision.
Everybody is used to the objects of vision being in front of their
face; hence everybody has a set towards thinking that such conditions hold, and that they can see that they hold, even when they
do not. Hence everybody will agree about what they seem to see
in a mirror.[1] If my explanation is correct, it would follow that if
everything we saw was seen by means of a mirror, then eventually
we should be able to shake off any vestige of illusion. The objects
seen would be seen as being where they really were.

The same sort of explanation could be applied to many other

---

[1] The fact that we can have photographs of mirror-images should not
worry us here. Photographs are made by light-waves striking a sensitive
surface, and in the case of a mirror-image the rays received on the surface are
just the same as if the object were where the mirror-image seems to be. Hence
it registers the same picture as if this were so. But *seeing* is different from taking photographs. We do not 'develop' our retina, and then scrutinise it to see
what the external world is like.

sensory illusions, although each different case requires a little in-genuity to work out the mechanism of deception. In the case of the 'bent stick', for example, in order to see the portion of the stick that is in water we must not turn our eyes directly towards it, as we normally do with physical objects. This is because the light-rays are bent, and do not, as they normally do, take a straight line from object to eye. But we continue to assume that viewing conditions are quite normal, and so the illusion arises.

However, this line of explanation cannot suffice to explain all types of sensory illusion. It could not explain after-images, for in-stance, or hallucinations. In these cases, other sorts of causal ex-planations must be attempted. But something has been done if such apparently public phenomena as mirror-images can be ex-plained away as only having the 'publicity' of a *general* deception, a deception due to the absence of certain conditions under which perception almost invariably takes place.

In this chapter we have tried to meet the Argument from Il-lusion by offering an analysis of sensory illusion which would escape the need to postulate an immediate object of perception in the case of sensory illusion. We said that in sensory illusion we merely *believe* or are inclined to believe that we are perceiving, veridically perceiving, some physical object or state of affairs. We also gave an analysis of what it is to have a sense-impression. It is to believe, or be inclined to believe, that we are *immediately* perceiving some physical object or state of affairs. Where 'the sense-impression corresponds to reality' the belief is true, where it does not, the belief is false. Correspondence or lack of corre-spondence of sense-impressions to reality is nothing but the truth or falsity of certain beliefs.

At no point in our analysis have we given any account of our two key terms 'perception' and 'belief'. These have been the unde-fined concepts in terms of which the analysis has proceeded. We have, however, insisted on giving 'perception' its ordinary use. That is to say, we have taken it that what is perceived must have physical existence. When we suffer an illusion we do not perceive, although we may *think* we perceive. If we have been successful, we have undercut the Argument from Illusion and have shown that it does not force us to embrace either of those Iron Maidens, Representationalism or Phenomenalism.

PART THREE

The Argument from Verification

8

THE ARGUMENT FROM
VERIFICATION

BUT we are still not yet done with the Argument from Illusion. The Phenomenalist may revive it in a rather different form, which we shall christen the 'Argument from Verification'.

Let us once again compare the two cases, first the man who really sees a cat, and second the man who has an hallucination as of a cat, an hallucination exactly like the veridical perception. In both these cases, we have argued, the percipients will believe or have a tendency to believe, that they are seeing a cat. In both cases they will believe, or have a tendency to believe, that they are *immediately* seeing the same sort of cat-like shape (in other language, they will have the same sense-impressions). But only in the first case will the beliefs (or inclinations to believe) involved be correct.

Now, confronted with this account, the Phenomenalist can still raise the old sceptical questions 'How do we know when we are really seeing?' 'How do we *sort out* veridical perception from sensory illusion?'[1]

The question seems to admit of no easy answer. As the Argument from Illusion has shown, and as we have admitted, there is

---

[1] The reason we do not find the Argument from Verification in Berkeley's writings is, no doubt, that he does not wish even to seem to be countenancing the sceptic. But in fact it is a very suitable argument for the Phenomenalist to use, for *Phenomenalism is parasitic upon scepticism*. The Phenomenalist first raises the sceptical difficulties, and then appears as the heaven-sent deliverer from them.

H

no intrinsic difference between veridical perception and sensory illusion. What is in fact veridical perception *could* be sensory illusion; what is in fact sensory illusion *could* be veridical perception. Where we see, it is logically possible that we could be incorrectly thinking we were seeing, and yet our sense-impressions, and everything else involved in the perceptual experience, remain exactly the same. It is no good saying that veridical perception corresponds with the physical facts. For how do we find out about the physical facts? Surely only by perception. But then the sceptical doubt can be raised again about any perception that we use in an endeavour to establish the correspondence to the physical facts.

On certain occasions we believe we are perceiving, but how do we know we are in fact perceiving? The experience exhibits no intrinsic marks of difference from sensory illusion. At this point we begin to feel that the problem is that of getting from the evidence of our senses, the perceptual experience, to physical reality. How can we make the jump?

But now the Phenomenalist will point out that the only way we could decide we were really perceiving is by using the test of *coherence*, by checking one perception against another, against our own perceptions and those of other people. If it looks to me now, feels to me now, smells to me now and tastes to me now, as if there is an orange on the mantelpiece on a certain occasion, and if it looks, feels, smells and tastes that way to everybody, then we know that there is an orange on the mantelpiece. This suggests that we should solve the sceptical problem by simply *identifying* the fact that there is an orange on the mantelpiece with everybody's perception 'of it'. If it seems to everybody as if they are perceiving an X, then they *are* perceiving an X. This answer may need to be sophisticated somewhat in order to deal with unobserved states of affairs, with cases where one's perceptions are never checked by oneself or others, and even with the logical possibility that the most coherent run of perceptions might be undermined by other perceptual evidence; but this will not alter the principle of the thing. In order to avoid scepticism, the veridical character of a veridical perception must be identified with its relations to other perceptions.

One might try to avoid this conclusion by distinguishing between having good reasons for asserting X, and the assertion of X itself.[1] If everybody's perceptions agree, if it seems to everybody that there is an orange on the mantelpiece on a certain occasion, then we have good reasons, the best of reasons, for asserting that there *is* an orange on the mantelpiece. But our good reasons for the assertion are not to be identified with the assertion itself.

In order to support this distinction, one might draw a parallel with knowledge of the future. One might have the best of reasons for thinking that it will not rain tomorrow in Melbourne, all the evidence that could possibly be desired. Everything might point towards saying that it will not rain tomorrow. Now in such circumstances it would certainly be profoundly irrational to admit the evidence, and yet assert that it *will* rain tomorrow in Melbourne. Yet however irrational, such an assertion would not involve *self-contradiction*, for the evidence about present states of affairs does not *entail* that it will not rain tomorrow. The present state of affairs and the state of affairs that will obtain tomorrow, are two different states of affairs, the one cannot be identified with the other in any way.

In just the same way, it might be suggested, if it seems to everybody that there is an orange on the mantelpiece on a certain occasion, and if no reason has been offered for doubting these perceptions, then it would be profoundly irrational to admit this evidence, and yet deny the conclusion that there *is* an orange on the mantelpiece. But the evidence is not *identical* with the conclusion, and so it would not be self-contradictory to admit the evidence and deny the conclusion. People's perceptions are something different from the object or state of affairs perceived.

But the Phenomenalist can quite well reply that the parallel is not a fair one. Although we may have the best possible evidence we can have *now* that it will not rain tomorrow, still we have not got *the best evidence possible*. The best evidence possible will be the perceptions of myself and others *tomorrow*. If it seems to us all to be fine, and if no other perceptual evidence is forthcoming to cast doubt on these perceptions, then and only then have we the best possible evidence. But in the case of the orange on the mantelpiece we already have the best evidence possible, viz. direct and corroborated perceptual evidence. If it is still said that, in the case

---

[1] At one stage I myself wished to take this way out. The error of my ways was shown to me by Professor D. A. T. Gasking, to whom I am greatly indebted for this section of my argument.

of the orange, the physical state of affairs is something quite distinct from the sensory evidence we have for it, we are putting physical reality beyond our sense-impressions, and are back with the sceptical problems of the Representative theory.

It seems to me that this argument is unanswerable, and that we cannot evade the Argument from Verification by distinguishing between having the best possible sensory reasons for asserting the occurrence of a certain physical state of affairs, and asserting the occurrence of that physical state of affairs.

But must we then accept Phenomenalism? It seems to me that the Phenomenalist has based his argument on the assumption that our perceptions are our *evidence* for the assertion of certain physical states of affairs.[1] And I grant that once this assumption is made the Phenomenalist conclusion is inevitable. But I think that this is not the true account of the relationship between perceptions and the physical world, and that once the real relationship is understood the Phenomenalist argument collapses.

But, in order to bring this point out, we shall have to undertake a large task, that of giving an analysis or account of what it is to perceive a physical object or state of affairs. So I propose to devote a chapter to an examination of the nature of perception, a task which is, in any case, of the greatest importance and interest in its own right. Having done this, we can return and answer the Argument from Verification.

[1] The Phenomenalist who uses the Argument from Verification need not say that the immediate object of perception is a sense-impression. But he will have to say that our immediate *evidence* for the truth of perceptual statements is our own sense-impressions or perceptual experience. This seems to come to much the same thing.

9

THE NATURE OF
PERCEPTION

IN chapter 7 we gave an analysis of sensory illusion. But the analysis made use of the concept of ordinary, veridical, perception. In
this chapter we attempt a further task, that of giving an account of
the nature of veridical perception itself. This will also permit a
deeper analysis of sensory illusion.

What is perception? A flood of light is thrown on this question
by asking 'What can somebody who can perceive do, that somebody who cannot perceive cannot do? What *powers* does perception add?' The answer is clear: a man who has his sight, for instance, has a way of discovering facts about his environment
which the blind man lacks. He can discover that there are hills in
the distance, or find out what are the forms and colours of the
painting before him, simply by turning his eyes towards these objects. The blind man has no such power. His knowledge of these
things, if he gains it at all, must come in a much more slow and
painful way. Perceiving then, that is, seeing, touching, hearing,
tasting and smelling, is a way of learning about what goes on
around us. To say of any organism that it can perceive is to imply
that it can acquire a certain amount of knowledge of the world
around it by means of certain organs called the senses. If the organism could not do this, we should not say that it could *perceive*.

These reflections suggest the thesis, which was hinted at in
Chapter 7, that perception is *nothing but* the acquiring of knowledge
of, or, on occasions, the acquiring of an inclination to believe in,
particular facts about the physical world, by means of our senses.

We have already offered an analysis of sensory illusion as a belief or inclination to believe that we are (veridically) perceiving something. A more profound analysis of sensory illusion may now be offered, corresponding to our proposed analysis of perception. To suffer sensory illusion is to acquire a false belief or inclination to a false belief in particular propositions about the physical world, by means of our senses.[1]

What exactly is meant by the phrase 'inclination to believe something about the physical world' here? In the first place it involves a certain thought or proposition about the physical world. For instance, it may involve the thought or proposition that there is a loud noise occurring now or that the cat is on the mat. In the second place this thought is a *presumptive thought*,[2] it is a thought which we would necessarily take as true but for the fact that we actually hold other beliefs about the world, beliefs which imply the falsity of this presumptive thought. It is a thought about the world that pushes towards being a belief, but is held back by other contradictory beliefs.

What becomes of the distinction between immediate and mediate perception if these formulae are accepted? I think we shall have to replace it by a distinction between beliefs about the world that are immediately acquired and beliefs mediately acquired, that is, suggested by the immediately acquired beliefs. When I hear a certain sound, I acquire immediately the belief that there is a sound occurring now; when I am said to hear a coach, the immediate belief that there is a sound occurring now *suggests* to me the further belief that there is a coach outside.

We shall now try to defend these theses by considering and refuting the objections that might be brought against them. It will be convenient to divide our defence into two parts. In the first part, we shall be concerned with arguments purporting to prove that perception does not always involve the acquiring of know-

---

[1] This is not absolutely accurate. On occasions I might acquire such a false belief or inclination to a false belief, even although my sense-organs had not been stimulated. But in such cases I would *believe or be inclined to believe* that my belief or inclination to believe something about the world was acquired by means of my senses. But in order not to send the reader insane, I will omit this qualification from my formula.

[2] I owe the phrase to Dr. A. C. Jackson. Such 'presumptive thoughts' are to be found in other fields besides perception, as we have mentioned in chap. 7, sec. 2.

ledge of, or inclination to believe in, particular facts about the physical world by means of our senses, together with the parallel thesis about sensory illusion. In the second part, we shall be concerned with arguments purporting to prove that, even if perception does involve the acquiring of such knowledge, it involves something more as well.

I. PERCEPTION ALWAYS INVOLVES THE ACQUIRING OF KNOWLEDGE OF PARTICULAR FACTS ABOUT THE PHYSICAL WORLD, BY MEANS OF THE SENSES

Objection 1(*a*): *Perception does not always give us a knowledge of FACTS.*[1]

Is the knowledge of the physical world acquired by perception always a knowledge of *facts*? There is no doubt that our senses are often means by which we come to know facts about our environment, means by which we learn that something is the case. I come into the room, and, as a result of turning my eyes in a certain direction, I learn that the cat is on the mat. Or we could put it by saying that as a result of using my eyes, I acquire knowledge of the truth of the statement 'the cat is on the mat'. Again, we could put it by saying that I *see that* the cat is on the mat. The accusative of a verb of perception is often a fact, or truth. But at other times the accusatives of verbs of perception seem not to be facts, but to be *things*. We see the mountain, feel the hot water, smell the flower, taste the pudding or hear the train. These locutions may seem to tell against our thesis by suggesting that, sometimes at least, perception is not a matter of acquiring knowledge of particular facts about the physical world. Things are not facts, and sometimes we are said to perceive things not facts.

This objection may be linked up with the distinction that is sometimes drawn between knowledge by acquaintance and merely descriptive knowledge or knowledge of truths. What perception gives us, it may be argued, is a direct acquaintance with certain objects. This acquaintance may give rise to a knowledge of particular facts about the physical world, but some perception, at least, involves mere acquaintance and no knowledge of facts.

But suppose that I am lying awake at night, and I hear a train.

[1] For the moment I will drop the tedious qualification 'or inclination to believe'.

Have I not gained the knowledge that there is at that moment a train in my environment, within ear-shot as we say? If I did not know that fact how could I possibly be said to hear the train? (Of course, I might simply hear a noise. But then I would at least have come to know that there was a noise occurring now.) I go into a room, and I smell a smell. Can it be denied that I now know that there is a smell in the room? And to know this is to know a fact about the world. If I did not know that there was a smell in the room, how could I be said to smell the smell? Hence it seems that, whenever we talk about perceiving things in our environment or talk about perceiving features of things, we can also talk of acquiring knowledge of particular facts about these things. To smell a smell in a room may not just be the coming to know that there is a smell in the room now, but this acquiring of knowledge of a fact is certainly involved in the perception. Even if our other senses were not operating so that we had no knowledge that we were in a room, or even where we were at all, we should still acquire this much knowledge: that a smell exists now.

The reason that we seldom feel called on to state these pieces of knowledge explicitly, but content ourselves with reporting that we heard a train, or smelled a smell, is fairly easy to see. If we smell a smell, our organs are so constituted that the smelly object or area must be quite close to our noses. If we hear a noise, our organs of hearing are so constituted that the noise must be at no very great distance from us. And so on. There is no need to report that there is a noise in my vicinity, for to say simply that I *heard* a noise carries this implication to anybody who knows anything about the way the ears operate.

Objection 1(b): Perception does not always involve the ACQUIRING of knowledge

But granting that perception must imply knowledge of particular facts about the physical world, need it always involve the *acquiring* of such knowledge? After all, sometimes we perceive *familiar* objects. Each day I see my gate in front of me as I walk up the path, but I cannot be said to acquire the knowledge that there is a brown gate in front of my house, because I already know this. Yet I certainly perceive a brown gate.

Now I am not absolutely sure that there is nothing in this objection. We might be forced to admit that in some cases perception involved some sort of coming-to-contemplate a known fact about the world, and not an acquiring of knowledge. But there are a number of points that can be made which, at the very least, reduce the importance of the objection.

In the first place, even though I may know a certain amount about my gate when I am not looking at it, yet, when my eyes are turned towards it, there will be very much more that I know about it than at other times. This will be shown by the fact that, while I am looking at it, there is much that I can say truly about it which I could not say when I am not looking at it. When looking at it, I may be able to say it has so many bars, that one bar is bent, that there is a jagged scratch on the paint of another bar, yet be able to say none of these things when I turn away. When I look at the gate I am, as it were, flooded with knowledge about the gate, knowledge which ebbs away when I stop looking.[1] Even in the case of the brown colour of my gate I may be quite unable to specify the *precise* shade unless I am actually looking at it. (It may be objected here that, even when I am looking at the gate and per-ceiving the precise shade of the colour, I may still not be able to *specify* the shade, because of an inadequate colour vocabulary. But I could still be said to know what the precise shade of colour was while I was looking at the gate, even though I did not know what its *name* was, because I would be able to pass certain tests. I could, for instance, note that the colour was identical with a certain shade in a colour chart. Failing the possibility of my noting this, or noting something like this, I could not be said to *perceive* just what was the precise shade of colour of the gate.)

Secondly, and still more importantly, we must distinguish be-tween facts about my gate in the past, and facts about my gate now, at the time I am looking at it. Before I look at my gate today what I *know* is that the gate has been brown in the past. I may be pretty sure that it is still brown, but it is possible that somebody has painted it a different colour during the night, or that some other misfortune has befallen it. It is always possible for the ob-jects in my environment to suffer change or destruction. So, when my eyes rest on my gate as I go out, I *can* be said to *acquire* knowledge, viz. that it is brown *now*, or that it is brown *still*. Per-ception normally gives us *up-to-the-moment* information about the

[1] Cf. Locke *Essay* Bk. II, chap. X, 4; who compares our perceptions to 'shadows . . . flying over fields of corn.'

physical world,[1] even if the information is only that things are just the same as they were the previous moment.

Finally, even if a case is constructed where we have such good grounds for believing that the gate will be brown when we look at it that we could properly be said to *know* the gate will be brown, nevertheless actual looking sets the seal on this assurance. This is shown by the fact that, if any doubt were raised about the colour of the gate, it would be to perception that we would appeal. So, even in such a case, we could say that, although we do not acquire knowledge, because we know already what the result of looking will be, nevertheless we do acquire a still more complete assurance of certain facts about our present environment.

The fact that perception involves, generally at least, an *acquiring* of knowledge about the physical world, enables us to understand Professor Ryle's contention that words like 'see', 'hear', etc., are 'achievement-words'. For to acquire knowledge is an achievement.[2]

Objection 1(c): Perception does not necessarily involve the use of sense-organs

We are arguing the thesis that perception must always involve the acquiring of knowledge of particular facts about the physical world, by means of our senses. In saying 'by means of our senses' we mean *only* that the having of those physical objects we call sense-organs, and their being in a certain condition, are empirically necessary preconditions for acquiring such knowledge. In order to see that the cat is on the mat my eyes must be in working order, and turned towards the cat. Nothing more mysterious is meant than these simple biological facts.

---

[1] Later we shall be considering arguments drawn from the 'time-lag' between the event perceived and the perceiving of it. Cf. chap. 11, sec. 2.

[2] Cf. 'Sensations' in *Contemporary British Philosophy* (*Third Series*) p. 442. '. . . finding out something by seeing and hearing is, so to speak, a success or victory in the game of exploring the world'. It is true that talk of achievements or victories may seem a rather inflated terminology for such a simple thing as perception. If this worries anybody, one could speak of 'getting' instead.

Notice that even if some perception only involves mere coming-to-contemplate facts already known, what it involves is a *coming* to do something, viz. contemplating.

Now it might be objected that the possession of sense-organs is not really necessary for perception. For although *in fact* perception may depend on sense-organs, we can quite well imagine persons who fulfil all the other criteria for being able to perceive, but who have nothing that can be identified as sense-organs. (They refer to facts about their environment, and have the same powers of discovering what is going on as ordinary perceivers have, but these powers are not correlated with the condition of any of their organs, at least in any obvious way.)

Now I do not wish to deal with this objection too dogmatically. The statement that perception requires sense-organs swings uneasily between being a merely conceptual statement, and being an empirical truth. I do not think we should be too zealous to push it one way or the other. All I wish to point out is that, whether empirical fact or logical necessity, it is appropriate to ask of somebody who perceives what he perceives *with*.[1] And the appropriate answer is to indicate some bodily organ or organs; the eyes, ears, tongue, nose, skin, etc.

This fact is important, because it helps to account for the special, 'flavour' of perception. When our sense-organs are operating, when our eyes are open, our ears cocked, when we are tasting, smelling or touching, we are not only acquiring knowledge of facts about our environment, but we also very often have certain characteristic *sensations* associated with the operation of each organ. (By 'sensation' here I do not mean the having of appropriate sense-impressions or sense-data. Here I am referring simply to bodily sensations, to feelings of strain involved in using the eye-muscles, ticklings of the nostrils, burnings of the tongue, pressures on the eardrums, tinglings of the skin, and things like that. In other words I am giving the word 'sensation' its *ordinary* use.[2])

Since the operation of our sense-organs normally produces certain sensations in them (although our attention to these sensations

[1] Even here we must note one exception: some perceptions of our own bodily states. I can tell that my hand is hot without naturally associating any sense-organ with this perception.

[2] Cf. our discussion of sensation in chap. 1. It is primarily what I called 'sensations proper' that I have in mind here. But the sensations may include sense-impressions of our bodily state. As we have pointed out, these have no organ naturally associated with them, so there is no danger of a vicious regress.

is often only marginal), perception is normally accompanied by certain bodily sensations. The existence of this contingent connection between perception and certain sorts of sensation may *help* to explain the special 'feel' of perception.

2. PERCEPTION IS NOTHING BUT THE ACQUIRING OF KNOWLEDGE OF PARTICULAR FACTS ABOUT THE WORLD, BY MEANS OF THE SENSES

I hope that I have now given good reasons for saying that perception necessarily involves the acquiring of knowledge of (or inclination to believe in) particular facts about the physical world, by means of our senses. We have allowed some doubts as to whether perception always involves the *acquiring* of such knowledge, and we have admitted that one could say, if one wanted to, that the use of the sense-organs was a merely contingent feature of perception. But with these reservations, our thesis stands. I have not bothered to offer a similar justification of the thesis that to suffer sensory illusion is to acquire a false belief, or inclination to a false belief, in particular propositions about the physical world, by means of our senses. The argument would follow the same track.

Objection 2(a): Perception seems much more than our thesis allows

One great difficulty about saying that perception is nothing but the acquiring of knowledge about the physical world by means of the senses is that it seems to involve so much more than this. Look at the difference between being told that there is a cat on the mat, either by someone one trusts completely or someone whom one is merely inclined to believe, and actually *seeing* it. Again, look at the difference between reaching a false belief or inclination to a false belief that there is a cat on the mat, and actually being *hallucinated*. Any theory must explain these differences, yet ours, it seems, fails to do so.

Now something has been done to answer this point in discussing objection 1(*b*) where we pointed out that in perception we are flooded with up-to-the-moment knowledge of the physical world, knowledge that we would not get except by perception. We have pointed out further, in discussing objection 1(*c*) that the operation of the sense-organs is accompanied by characteristic *sensations*, which give the activity of perception something of a special flavour. But still more can be said.

When I perceive the cat is on the mat, I am normally not only aware that the cat is on the mat, but I am *also* aware that I am perceiving the cat.[1] If I am asked how it is that I am aware that the cat is on the mat I can reply that I know by using my eyes. Originally this is something that has to be found out, for it is a contingent fact that opening our eyes can give us knowledge of the shapes and colours of things around us. (The discovery is made by closing our eyes and discovering that we are then unable to acquire knowledge of these properties of things, then opening them and finding the power restored. It is an application of the methods of difference and agreement.) Nevertheless, this is something that we quickly become aware of, so that in ordinary perception we not only acquire the knowledge that the cat is on the mat, but we also know that it is by means of our eyes that we have this knowledge. We can report that the cat is on the mat, and we can report that we can *see* that the cat is on the mat. And we will also be vaguely aware of the characteristic sensations in the eye that go with looking.

Now in the case of hallucinations we find the same sort of thing. Not only do we acquire the false belief (or inclination to believe) that there is a cat on the mat, but we also have the false belief (or inclination to believe) that we are actually *seeing* the cat, using our eyes to discover it is there. And, of course, it will usually be true that our eyes will be open, and pointing to the place where the imaginary cat is supposed to be, and we will have those sensations in the eyes which are characteristic of focusing our eyes on an object at that distance from them.[2]

So I suggest that we can explain the likeness between perception and hallucination, and their difference from mere acquiring true and false beliefs, or inclinations to believe, without abandoning the essentials of our thesis. In the case of perception I not only acquire the knowledge that the cat is on the mat, but I also know that I have used my eyes to acquire this knowledge. That is to say, I not only acquire the knowledge that the cat is on the mat,

[1] Cf. chap. 7, sec. 1.

[2] Although this need not occur. We can have peculiar cases of hallucination where we seem to ourselves to be seeing, even although our eyes are not open at all.

but I also know that I have come to know it *by seeing*. (And, incidentally, the actions of my eyes will be accompanied by characteristic sensations.) This is more than mere acquiring of knowledge about the world, but what is more is only the *further* knowledge of the way the knowledge about the world was acquired. In the case of hallucination I acquire the false belief, or inclination to believe, that the cat is on the mat, and am also under the impression, or at any rate am inclined to believe, that it is by using my eyes, that is, by seeing, that I came to this putative knowledge. (And I *may* be thus far right: my eyes may be open, focused on that spot, and I may have sensations in the eyes.) This is more than a mere false belief, or inclination to a false belief, about the physical world. But what is more is a belief, or inclination to believe, that this belief, or inclination to believe, was acquired in a certain way.

We could now offer a slight modification of our thesis. Perception, we could now say, is the acquiring knowledge of, or inclination to believe in, particular facts about the physical world, by means of our senses, *normally accompanied by knowledge of the means*. And to suffer sensory illusion, we could say, is to acquire a false belief or inclination to a false belief in particular propositions about the physical world, by means of our senses, *normally accompanied by the belief or inclination to believe that the belief or inclination to believe something about the world is acquired by means of the senses*. But having noted these modifications we may omit them in future statements of our thesis, because of the inconvenience of such long formulae.

We have now pointed to three differentiating marks of the *perceptual* acquiring of knowledge of, or inclinations to believe in, particular facts about the world. In the first place it is characterised by a flood of up-to-date information about our environment, in the second place it is accompanied by characteristic sensations in the organs of perception, and in the third place it normally involves knowledge of the means by which this knowledge is acquired, viz. the operation of the sense organs.

But it will still be objected that this is not all there is to perception. When I see a cat before me, and believe my eyes; when I see a cat before me, but fail to believe my eyes; when I have the hallucination of a cat before me, and believe my eyes; when I have the hallucination of a cat before me, but do not believe my eyes; in all these cases it will be urged, apart from beliefs or inclinations to believe that there is a cat before me, and apart from beliefs that, or inclinations to believe that, these beliefs or inclinations to believe are acquired by means of my eyes, there is that on which these beliefs or inclinations to believe are *grounded*, the *visual experience* which marks off these cases from cases where only beliefs or inclinations to believe are in question.

The reply to this objection must take the same lines as our reply to the similar objection to our analysis of sensory illusion in Chapter 7, sec. 3. There we examined the view that there were two distinct elements involved in sensory illusion: (i) the false belief, or inclination to believe falsely, that we are perceiving a certain physical object or state of affairs; (ii) the sense-impression on which this belief is founded. We argued against this distinction by saying that if the sense-impression was no mere accompaniment or cause of the belief, or inclination to believe, that we are perceiving, but rather was that on which the belief, or inclination to believe, was *founded*; then the relationship between the two must be either that having the sense-impression *entailed* having the belief or inclination to believe that we are perceiving, or else that there was a contingent connection known to hold between the two. But if the relationship is one of entailment or necessary connection, then the sense-impression already involves the belief or inclination to believe that we are perceiving, which is contrary to the hypothesis. If however the relationship is *not* one of entailment, the question arises why having a certain sense-impression should give us any grounds for a belief, or inclination to believe, that we are perceiving a certain physical state of affairs. The only answer to this can be that this sort of sense-impression is *generally* found associated with a certain physical state of affairs, so that the sense-impression is *normally* a good guide to the nature of physical reality. But how do we know it is a good guide? For, on the hypothesis being examined, we have no way of getting at physical reality save via the sense-impression. Hence we are inevitably led to Phenomenalism, an *identification* of physical reality with normal or coherent sense-impressions. But since we had already advanced conclusive reasons for rejecting Phenomenalism, we had to give up the distinction between a false belief or inclination to a false belief that we are perceiving a certain state of affairs, and the sense-impression on which the false belief or inclination to a false belief is supposed to be grounded.

Exactly the same line of argument must be adopted here. We are now proposing an analysis of perception itself in terms of the acquiring of knowledge of, or inclination to believe in, particular facts about the world. If it is said that perception involves 'perceptual experience' over and above this, the first question must be whether this perceptual experience is a mere accompaniment and/or cause of the knowledge or inclination to believe, or is its *ground*. If the former alternative is chosen, we may admit the possibility of such accompanying experiences, but must insist that the experiences have nothing to do with our knowledge of the physical world. They would be a mere phenomenological curiosity. But I take it that it would be the second possibility that would be preferred, that the 'perceptual experience' is supposed to underpin in some way, to serve as a ground for, the beliefs that we arrive at about the physical world. But there can be no necessary connection between the perceptual experience, and the beliefs or inclinations to believe in something about the world that we arrive at as a result of the experience. For a necessary connection would imply that the perceptual experience was nothing distinct from, that it already involved, the beliefs or inclinations to believe. But to underpin the beliefs, or inclinations to believe, it must be distinct from them. And then the question arises why the perceptual experience gives any justification for the beliefs, or inclinations to believe. In order to be justified in passing from the perceptual experience to a certain belief about physical reality, we should have to know that certain perceptual experiences generally occurred when a certain state of affairs obtained in the physical world. But to know this, we would have to gain independent knowledge of the physical world; and if perceptual experience is the basis of our knowledge of the world, this cannot be done.

Once again we are faced with the choice of making physical reality inaccessible behind a screen of experiences, or else identifying physical reality with the experiences: that is we are faced with a choice between the Representative or the Phenomenalist theory. Both these theories we have claimed to refute. And so we are forced to reject the view that our belief, or inclination to believe, in something about the physical world (which is certainly *involved* in all perception, as we showed earlier) is grounded on further 'perceptual experience'. Despite its initial attractions, the view leads to unacceptable consequences.

Objection 2(b): Some acquiring of knowledge of particular facts about the physical world by means of the senses is not perception

Suppose I am handed cards which tell me what is going on behind my back. Here I acquire knowledge of a fact about my environment, and, what is more, I acquire this knowledge by means of my senses (looking at the words on the cards). Yet, it may be said, we would not call this *perceiving* what is going on behind my back. Hence it seems that our analysis of the nature of perception is, at the very least, incomplete.

But in fact it is not at all clear that we should not be prepared to treat this acquiring of knowledge of what is going on behind my back as a case of perception. It is certainly not a case of *immediate* perception, but can we not say it is a case of *mediate* perception, like hearing a coach while seated indoors? After all, we would say that we *saw* that a certain happening had taken place behind our back. And if we had not been handed cards, but had been told what was happening, we would say that we *heard* that certain things were going on behind our back.

Nevertheless, it may be replied, this is not enough, because although we should be prepared to say that we saw (or heard) *that* a certain happening had taken place, we should not be prepared to say that we *saw the happening*, in the way that we *would* be prepared to say that we heard a coach. It may be true, as was argued in answer to objection 1(b) that, wherever we can say that we hear a coach we can also say that we can hear *that* there is a coach nearby. But the converse does not hold. And, it will be argued, we can only speak of perception where we can speak of perceiving *things* or features of things.

However, if I use my eyes to acquire certain knowledge of facts about the physical world, and if we are prepared to use the word 'see' in such a case, there can be no real reason to deny that this is a case of (mediate) perception. After all, the use of the word 'see' is not *metaphorical* here, as it is when we are said to 'see' the point of an argument. Nevertheless, it is true that there is a residual problem. What marks off the cases where we are prepared to say we perceive things or features of things, from the cases where we are only prepared to say we perceive *that* something is the case?

I am not sure what to say here, but will offer the following suggestion. As we noted in answer to objection 1(*b*) we are prepared to say simply that we hear a train, and do not go to the trouble of saying that we hear *that* there is a train somewhere not too far away from us, because anybody who knows anything about the way ears operate knows that a heard train must be not too far away from the ear that hears it. Perhaps, then, we speak of seeing *things* (or features of things) only in the cases where our deep familiarity with the way the sense-organs operate, and the way the world goes, enables us to dispense with comparatively elaborate formulae like 'I perceive that . . .'. It is worth noticing here that immediate perception can always be spoken of as perception of *things* or features of things. Now we know how the sense-organs operate, and so we can *easily* expand such statements of immediate perception into statements that such-and-such is the case in our environment. In the case of hearing a train, this is only mediate perception, but the passage from the immediate perception of the sound to the mediate perception of the train is so easy and familiar, and the sound and the train are so intimately connected, that we can afford to speak simply of hearing the train. But, in the case of the cards which tell us what is happening behind our back, there is not the same intimacy of connection between the immediate perception of the visual characteristics of the card, and the mediate perception of the situation behind my back. Hence we only say that we see *that* certain things are the case. If this suggestion be correct, the perception of things, or the features of things, is not to be opposed to perceiving *that* something is the case. For it is simply a special case of perceiving *that*.

Objection 2(*c*): *Animals and children may have perceptions without beliefs about the physical world.*

It may be objected now that our analysis is only plausible because we have restricted ourselves to the consideration of those who have had some skill and practice in using their sense-organs. But what about newly-born children or animals, or persons born blind and later made to see? Will they not have perceptions? Yet their perceptions may well be far too inchoate and confused to give rise to any beliefs about the physical world. And even we who have learned to use our sense-organs, may, on occasions, have utterly vague and confused perceptions, for instance, when coming out of an anaesthetic. Hence it seems that perception is more than we have allowed.

Now there is no doubt at all that perception can be inchoate and confused. But what hinders a *belief* from being inchoate and confused? We have not committed ourselves to the view that perception invariably involves *definite* and *explicit* judgements that certain things are the case in the physical world. It may well involve something very much less, something much less self-conscious and much more vague, and yet still describable as the acquiring of knowledge, belief, or inclination to believe, that something is the case in the physical world.

However elementary, however inchoate and confused, perception will surely involve some discrimination (whether correct or incorrect) of features of the environment. And to make a discrimination seems at the very least to *involve* coming to some belief about the environment.

This objection, however, may lead on to another. We say we can see something clearly, or that we can only see it dimly. Yet our acquiring of knowledge about the physical world by means of our senses could not be clear or dim.[1]

There seems to be little in this further objection. If we see a thing dimly we are unable to make out as many features of the thing as we can when we see clearly. Or, if we can make out as many features as we can normally, we cannot be so sure of our judgement as we can in normal conditions. It is clear that it would be quite easy to accommodate these possibilities within the framework of our analysis.

Objection 2(d): Our thesis leaves perceptual knowledge without a foundation

But, it may be objected, we think of the beliefs about our environment that perception yields us as constituting *knowledge*, perhaps indeed as constituting the whole foundation of our knowledge about the physical world. Now how can we say that perception ever yields knowledge, unless there is some ground or basis for our perceptual judgements? Our analysis, which reduces

---

[1] Cf. Plato *Theaetetus* 165d. Although Plato does not accept the thesis that 'perception is knowledge', he does not seem to think much of this particular objection.

perception simply to judgements about the physical world, leaves these judgements hanging, lacking the support that *knowledge* demands.

Now, in the case of mediate perception, we can *perhaps* say that it is grounded on our immediate perception. I can say I hear a coach because I immediately hear a certain sort of sound. But what of immediate perception? We can no doubt discover the *causes*, physical, physiological and psychological, of our immediate perceptions. But causes are not grounds, and such a causal account would do nothing to provide the support for our immediate perceptions that seems to be necessary if we are to reduce immediate perception to judgement, and yet still treat it as yielding us *knowledge*.

We shall have to say something more about this point when we come to give our answer to the Argument from Verification. Here we may point out that this objection rests on a completely false view of the nature of knowledge. It rests on the view that we only have knowledge where we have true belief, together with *good reasons* for this belief. This view is untenable, as Plato pointed out in the *Theaetetus*,[1] because these good reasons must again be things that we *know*, and so, on pain of an infinite regress, we cannot produce good reasons indefinitely. There must be at least some truths that we know *without* good reasons. And since immediate perception is, avowedly, the court of last appeal when it comes to questions about physical reality, there is no objection, it seems, to saying that in immediate perception at least, we acquire knowledge of certain facts about the physical world without good reasons. Error, that is to say, immediate perceptual illusion, may be always logically possible (this is the real point of Descartes' deceitful demon), but in many cases we know that it has not occurred.

This answer, it is true, gives a new handle to the sceptic. He can ask how it is that, lacking good reasons, we are able to pick out our true beliefs from our errors. How do we know that we know? But I shall leave this problem aside for the present. It will come up again in our reconsideration of the Argument from Verification.

I have now defended my account of perception against various objections. Perception, I have said, is the acquiring knowledge of,

[1] 206E—210B.

or inclination to believe in, particular facts about the physical world, by means of the senses. And to suffer sensory illusion is to acquire a false belief, or inclination to a false belief, in particular propositions about the physical world by means of the senses.[1]

My account may be called a *reductive* account because the concept of perception is shown to be a complex concept, definable in terms of such concepts as knowledge, belief and inclination to believe. The latter three, together with the concept of sensation, which finds an incidental employment in the course of the analysis, are the only specifically *mental* concepts in the proposed account. They have been treated as unanalysed terms, and no attempt made to give an account of any of them. It is to be noted, therefore, that no particular theory of the nature of knowledge, belief or sensation is pre-supposed.[2] It must be admitted, however, that these concepts provide very difficult problems, and that an analysis or other account of their nature might in some degree force us to revise the analysis of the nature of perception, or at any rate force us to see it in a new light.

I pause, however, to forestall one misunderstanding that may easily occur. Many modern philosophers hold that we must give a *dispositional* analysis of belief. If A believes p at time T, this does not imply that there is any psychical event occurring in A at time T. All that is implied is that *in some circumstances* A would act or speak in a certain way, or think certain thoughts. Now we have given an analysis of perception in terms of belief, and so it may seem that we are making perception a dispositional affair. Yet surely perception is an *event*?

Now, I have a great deal of sympathy with this account of belief, and I should myself think it a serious matter if it clashed with my analysis of perception. But there is, in fact, no clash at all. Granting, for the sake of argument, that a dispositional analysis of belief is correct, the *acquiring* of a belief may still be an event. The brittleness of a glass at time T is a dispositional property of the glass. But if the glass *acquires* the dispositional property of brittleness at time T, that acquiring is an event. And if it is pointed out that perception is an event of which we are *conscious*, I reply

[1] Minor qualifications and additions to these formulae have been mentioned in the course of the chapter, but are here omitted for the sake of simplicity.

[2] However, we have *excluded* certain views of the nature of knowledge in the course of this chapter.

that I see no difficulty in being conscious of acquiring a belief, even if we give a dispositional analysis of the nature of belief. (We shall, however, say something about *unconscious* perception in the next chapter.) So the analysis of perception defended in this chapter is compatible with a dispositional, as well as with a non-dispositional, account of belief.

This account of perception is to be contrasted with the view that appears, implicitly or explicitly, in most of the classical philosophers. Kant opposes intuition and conception, and says that, although both may be necessary for knowledge, yet they are nevertheless quite distinct. He is, I think, opposing perception, the faculty of sense, (conceived of as the having of sense-impressions or intuitions), to the forming of concepts and the arriving at judgements, the faculty of understanding. Kant understands Leibniz as trying to break down this distinction between perceiving and judging, and we too have been making the same attempt, for on our view to perceive is only to come to judge[1] that something is the case. The difficulties of the Kantian type of separation have gradually become more and more manifest to modern philosophers. We have attempted to show that perception is a sub-species of coming to judge, and to state what are the differentiating characteristics of the sub-species.

[1] The word 'judge' may be misleading here, because it may suggest that the acquiring of beliefs in perception is invariably a highly self-conscious and intellectual affair. The reverse is, of course, true. Animals perceive, and so, on my view, they acquire beliefs.

10

CONSEQUENCES OF OUR ACCOUNT OF THE NATURE OF PERCEPTION

WE are now in a position to answer the Argument from Verification. But before we do so, let us first look at some corollaries and consequences of our account of the nature of perception.

I. THE EXISTENCE OF UNCONSCIOUS PERCEPTION

Consider the following case. I am driving along an unfamiliar street, and I pass a hoarding. When I reach the end of the street I am asked what it was that the hoarding was advertising. *To my surprise* I am able to answer; to my surprise, because I was not conscious of seeing what was on the hoarding when I passed it, I did not notice it at the time. Should we say, nevertheless, that I *did* see it? There is no doubt that light-waves from the hoarding stimulated my retina and brain-centres, and that if this had not occurred I would not have known what the hoarding was advertising, but did I *see* the advertisement?

I think it follows from our analysis of perception that this case must count as seeing. For here I acquired knowledge of particular facts about the world by means of my eyes: the question put to me revealed that I knew something that I did not know before. (Of course, my possession of the knowledge may have been short-lived. If I had been asked the same question two blocks further on, I might not have known the answer.) There seems no reason to

123

object to the possibility of acquiring knowledge *unconsciously*. If up to a certain instant I am unable to answer question q, but if we have good reasons to believe that after that instant I could have answered q correctly, even although I did not realise *at* that instant that I had this new power, we seem to have a case of acquiring knowledge.

If this answer is found disturbing, then we could legislate that the acquiring of knowledge involved in perception must be a *conscious* acquiring, something we notice at the time. And then we would have to find a name to describe what happens in the case of the hoarding. But I think this would be an act of legislation, and that it is more natural to say that in such a case we really did see the advertisement on the hoarding, but were not *conscious* of seeing it.

What should we say about so-called 'subliminal perception'? A notice saying 'Eat ice-cream' is flashed on to the picture-screen, much too fast to see it, as we say. In the interval I buy an ice-cream—contrary to my wont. Should we say I really saw it, unconsciously? This seems incorrect, for I gained no knowledge about my environment, but only a desire to eat ice-cream. It is not like the case of the hoarding. Nevertheless, my sense-organs were stimulated, and it was *as if* I saw the notice, and was influenced by it. Perhaps it is best to say that this case has a 'family-resemblance' to unconscious perception, and leave it at that.

2. ARE THERE INTERMEDIATE CASES BETWEEN VERIDICAL AND ILLUSORY PERCEPTIONS?[1]

Perception, we have argued, normally involves the acquiring of knowledge. Sensory illusion, we have also argued, involves acquiring false belief or inclination to false belief. Between knowledge and false belief lies the sort of true belief that we would not be prepared to count as *knowledge*. This suggests that it is at least possible that there should be something intermediate between perception and sensory illusion.

Suppose somebody has perceptions which in fact correspond to reality, but suppose we have good reasons to believe that he would have had these perceptions whether or not the object

[1] The interesting possibility I cite here was pointed out to me by Dr. C. B. Martin.

'perceived' existed. Should we say he really perceives the object, or that he has an hallucination which corresponds with reality? This seems to be an intermediate or 'conflict' case. If our analysis of perception is correct, he acquires a true belief about his environment. We should hesitate to describe him as hallucinated, because hallucination entails *false* belief or an inclination to false belief. Yet it is also unattractive to describe the case as one of veridical perception, at any rate on our view of perception, because it is the sort of belief that we should not like to describe as 'knowledge'. We could, if we wanted to, *force* it either into the category of veridical perception, or else into the category of hallucination. But it seems better to do neither, and so to recognize it as a genuine intermediate case.

Dr. Martin has pointed out to me that this curious intermediate case casts light on the nature of ordinary veridical perception. In the intermediate case, the sense-impression corresponds with reality, but it is not *brought into existence by that reality*. It seems to be part of our concept of veridical perception that the perception should be the *causal result* of the operation of the thing perceived. This is one of the ideas that underlies the Representative theory of perception, although conjoined with the misleading conception that sense-impressions stand between us and physical reality. Later in this chapter we shall notice that the Representative theory embodies a second, even more important, insight, along with its errors.

3. REFORMULATION OF THE EMPIRICIST THEORY OF THE WAY WE ACQUIRE EMPIRICAL CONCEPTS[1]

We find in the thought of John Locke, and in Empiricist thought generally, a certain picture of the way we come by such concepts as 'ball', 'loud', 'to the left of', and other empirical concepts.

According to this view we begin with the *perception* of particular things, and then proceed to form *concepts* by abstracting from the perceived particulars. We are then in a position to weld these concepts together to form *judgements*. Perception, concept-formation, and judging are distinct activities even if, in developed

---

[1] The points made in this and the next section of the chapter were suggested to me by Professor H. H. Price.

perception, they are found inextricably intertwined with each other.

It is clear that we must reject this picture if our account of perception is correct. There can be no question of distinguishing a first stage, 'perception', from a third stage, 'judgement', because perception is the acquiring of knowledge ('judging') right from the start. And since the forming of judgements involves the possession of concepts, perception must also involve concepts right from the start.

At this point the problem may be raised where we originally get our concepts from. It cannot be from perception which already involves concepts.

The answer, I think, must be that there is no process of acquiring concepts before we acquire knowledge that something is the case in the physical world, because judgements are not *built up* out of concepts. Concepts, we must say, are *abstractions from judgements*, 'predicates of possible judgements' in the Kantian phrase. In our acquiring our first knowledge of our environment we acquire our first concepts, and we could not acquire concepts before this, because concepts are nothing outside judgements. There is not the space in this work to offer a detailed theory of the nature of judgement and the nature of concepts. But since an account of concepts as 'predicates of possible judgements' finds favour in modern philosophy, we shall excuse ourselves with these brief remarks.

But, if we take this line, it may be asked what becomes of the Empiricist contention that all our concepts are derived from *experience*? The answer is that it will have to be translated into the contention that all our concepts are derived from the acquisition of knowledge of particular facts about the world gained by means of our senses. The status of *this* contention would then have to be investigated further, but this is a topic that lies beyond the scope of the present work.

4. THE DISTINCTION BETWEEN SENSORY ILLUSION AND HALLUCINATION

Our account of perception enables us to give a very simple account of the difference between mere sensory illusion (the stick looking bent, the water feeling colder than it really is, etc.), and hallucination ('seeing' a cat that is not there). On our view, all perception, whether veridical or non-veridical, involves the acquiring of a belief, or inclination to believe, in an *existential* proposition to the effect that a certain particular object has a certain property or properties. It is of the form $(\exists x)\phi x.\psi x$. Now in all cases of non-veridical perception this proposition is *false*. But in mere sensory illusion it is true that the particular which is the subject of the proposition does exist. There really is a stick, even if it is not bent. There really is water in contact with my skin, even if I am wrong about how hot it is. Error is involved only in the property or properties that we assign to the particular. (The term 'property' here is, of course, to be understood widely. It might be some *relation* to another particular.) But, in the case of hallucination, the false belief that we hold, or are inclined to hold, involves a much more radical error. The particular that we take to exist, or are inclined to take to exist, has not just got different properties from the ones we take it to have, rather it does not exist at all. It is not that the cat on the mat is not black, there is no cat on the mat at all.

This classification is perhaps not absolutely rigid, but might admit of intermediate cases. In the case of mirror-images, for instance, we said at one stage that when we look at a mirror, we perceive *ourselves*, but that we perceive ourselves subject to certain distortions, in particular, subject to a distortion of place. If we took this line we would classify mirror-images among sensory illusions. But one might maintain that a thing's place at a particular time was so essential a part of the concept of the thing that mirror-images should rather be classified as a sort of hallucination, as the false belief or inclination to believe that there is a thing like me, but other than me, behind the surface of the glass. I am inclined to say that it does not matter which of these two things we say here.

5. THE NATURE OF SENSE-IMPRESSIONS

In chapter 7, sec. 3 we gave an account of the nature of sense-impressions by using the distinction between immediate and mediate perception. This distinction was explained still earlier (chapter 2) by reference to Berkeley's example of hearing a coach. The sound the coach makes is immediately heard, but the coach is only mediately heard, inferred from, or, better, *suggested by* what is immediately heard. (We pointed out further that the same sort of distinction can be drawn in the case of all the other senses.) It was then argued in chapter 7 that to have a sense-impression was to have a belief, or inclination to believe, that we were *immediately* perceiving something: a belief or inclination to believe we were hearing certain sounds, seeing objects of a certain shape and colour, feeling something hot, etc., while abstracting from the truth or falsity of such beliefs or inclinations to believe. And in view of the fact that we have accepted the possibility of *unconscious* perception, we now must add to this analysis by making it a matter of *conscious* belief or inclination to believe that we are immediately perceiving something. For in chapter 4 we refused to admit the possibility of having sense-impressions that we were not conscious of having.

But now we have offered an analysis of what it is to perceive, and along with this analysis a deeper account of the distinction between immediate and mediate perception. To perceive immediately, we have suggested, is to acquire by means of the senses knowledge of particular facts about the physical world, but a knowledge that is not mediated or suggested to us by any other knowledge of particular facts acquired by means of the senses. We may call it immediate knowledge, and distinguish it from the mediate knowledge which is acquired in mediate perception. A parallel account can be given of immediate and mediate sensory illusion. To speak of our sense-impressions, therefore, will be to speak of our conscious acquirings of immediate beliefs or inclinations to believe in particular propositions about the physical world, by means of our senses, without considering whether these propositions are true or false.

Our sense-impressions, therefore, are simply our conscious acquirings of impressions of the physical world by means of our senses, that is, they are conscious acquirings of beliefs or inclinations to believe in something about the world. But they are confined to those beliefs (inclinations to believe) which are 'immediate' in the sense which we have described. To take them as the *evidence* for our immediate beliefs or inclinations to believe in something about the world is to suffer from 'metaphysical double-vision', it is to take the same thing twice over.

We shall now show that this analysis of the nature of sense-impressions accounts for all sorts of features of sense-impressions, including those puzzling features of sense-impressions that we left unexplained in chapter 4. All these features of sense-impressions are in fact features of what is acquired when we have sense-impressions. In other words, they are features of *beliefs*.

(i) In the first place, we cannot be mistaken about the nature of our sense-impressions at the time of having them; our conscious beliefs or inclinations to believe are also things about which we cannot be mistaken at the time of holding them. (ii) In the second place, our sense-impressions are not directly under the control of our will, we cannot help having the sense-impressions that we have. Our beliefs, or inclinations to believe, are not under the direct control of our will either.[1] (iii) In the third place, it makes no sense to ask of either sense-impressions or beliefs where they are located in physical space.

These resemblances between sense-impressions and beliefs are not very important by themselves. They are shared by other mental phenomena, for example, emotions and dreams. But there are much more striking similarities to be discovered.

(iv) We noted in our discussion of sense-impressions in chapter 4 that, if we accept 'Hume's Principle' that our sense-impressions are as they appear to be (a principle that we argued *ought* to be accepted), we must go on to say that sense-impressions can be more, or less, precise and determinate. It may be impossible in principle to specify the *precise* shade of colour of a visual sense-impression that we have on a certain occasion, but on another occasion such specification may be perfectly possible. *Now beliefs or inclinations to believe can also be more, or less, precise and determinate.*[2] For suppose I have a belief about something I am *not* perceiving, for example, suppose I believe that a piece of cloth behind my back is coloured red. It is quite possible that I may have no opinion at all about its precise shade of colour, all that I may believe is that it is red. My belief may then be said to be imprecise or *indeterminate* in this respect. Alternatively, I might believe that the piece of cloth was of a certain quite precise shade, and then we could say that my belief was *determinate* in this respect. This determinacy or indeterminacy of beliefs seems to be the same thing as the determinacy or indeterminacy of sense-impressions.

Now in chapter 4 we found it a strange and puzzling thing to have to say that sense-impressions can be indeterminate in char-

---

[1] This resemblance was pointed out to me by Mr. D. L. Gunner.
[2] This resemblance was pointed out to me by Mr. D. C. Stove.

acter. Surely a thing must have a perfectly definite character; surely it cannot be indeterminate in nature? But there is nothing at all puzzling about the indeterminacy of a belief, or inclination to believe; and once we see that sense-impressions are nothing but the acquirings of beliefs, or inclinations to believe, our puzzlement vanishes. What we have instead is a striking verification of our account of the nature of sense-impressions.

(v) This is the place to clear up the problem also left over from chapter 4, of the intransitivity of similarity in the case of sense-impressions. The problem, it will be remembered, came up in the following form. Take three objects which differ very slightly in a certain respect, say colour. Comparison of A and B may furnish sense-impressions which are *identical* with respect to colour, comparison of B and C may also furnish sense-impressions which are *identical* with respect to colour, yet comparison of A and C may furnish sense-impressions which differ slightly with respect to colour. This seems impossible if sense-impressions are a sort of (non-physical) *thing*, but is easily explained on our view.

When we look at A and B we acquire an inclination to believe (falsely) that they are exactly the same colour. When we look at B and C we also acquire an inclination to believe (falsely) that they are exactly the same colour. But when we compare A and C we acquire an inclination to believe (truly) that they are slightly different in colour. In other words we are inclined to believe p and q which together entail r, and yet we are also inclined to believe not-r. This sort of thing is quite frequent in our mental life, and not at all puzzling. Our account of the nature of sense-impressions, therefore, once again explains the apparently inexplicable.

The reason why we trust our perceptual comparison of A and C, and so believe that there are slight but unperceivable colour-differences between A and B, and between B and C, is quite simple. We know that when things resemble each other very closely the fact they look exactly the same is by no means a good reason for thinking they *are* exactly the same. But when things look different, it is highly probable that they really are different. So we think A and C are really different in colour, and are then forced to conclude that B is slightly different in colour from both A and C, although we cannot perceive the difference.

(vi) In the sixth place, we have the idea that, in genuine perception, our sense-impressions 'correspond with reality', while in perceptual illusion they fail so to correspond. (It is one of the many implausibilities of Phenomenalism that it is unable to give this 'correspondence with reality' anything but a Pickwickian sense.) The Representative theory can account for this correspondence, for it treats the sense-impressions as a sort of picture or representation of the physical world.[1] But, even on the Representative theory, the 'correspondence with reality' that sense-impressions have is something *external to their own nature*. A picture is only a picture if it is *used* as a picture; in itself it is just an object, and the picture-function is external to it. The Representative theory therefore has to introduce something more than the sense-impressions, viz. a *belief* that the sense-impression is a true representation of reality. Only then can it say that the sense-impression corresponds to, or fails to correspond to, the physical world. But the difficulty with this view is that we have the feeling that sense-impressions have an *intrinsic* correspondence or lack of correspondence to physical reality.[2]

Now the indentification of sense-impressions with acquirings of beliefs explains and justifies this feeling. For beliefs *intrinsically* correspond or fail to correspond to reality. The correspondence or failure of correspondence to reality of our sense-impressions is therefore the same correspondence or failure of correspondence that our belief that there are mountains on the other side of the moon has to the actual facts.

Nor does this mean that our beliefs stand between us and physical reality, as sense-impressions do on the Representative theory. If they did, they would require further beliefs that they were correct representations of reality. In saying that our sense-impressions are acquirings of beliefs, and that they correspond or fail to correspond to physical reality, we therefore do nothing to depart from a Direct Realism.

(vii) Finally, our account of sense-impressions is able to explain the absence of a sharp gap between immediate and mediate perception. The absence of this gap was noted in Chapter 2, where we pointed out that it is easy to produce cases where we would

---

[1] This is the second important insight encapsulated in the Representative theory.

[2] Some philosophers have tried to express this apparent feature of sense-impressions by talking about the way sense-impressions 'point beyond themselves' to physical reality.

be hard put to decide whether a certain perception was immediate or mediate (e.g. the perception of the roundness of the moon).

We have argued that both our immediate perceptions (that is, our sense-impressions), and also our mediate perceptions, are nothing but the acquiring of beliefs about the world by means of our senses. The only difference between them is that in immediate perception the beliefs are acquired 'immediately', while in mediate perception they are suggested by the immediately acquired beliefs. We should therefore expect that there would be no sharp gap between the two sorts of perception. Since they are both acquirings of beliefs, it is natural that they should shade off into each other.

We might even turn the point round, and make it a positive argument for our account of sense-impressions. To perceive something mediately seems clearly to be nothing but an acquiring of beliefs. When I immediately hear a certain sort of sound, and then say that I hear a coach, it seems clear that all that happens is that I acquire the belief that there is a coach in my vicinity. But if mediate perception is nothing but the acquiring of beliefs, and it shades off into immediate perception, it is very natural to suppose that immediate perception is also nothing but the acquiring of beliefs. But to talk about sense-impressions, we have argued, is to talk of our immediate perceptions, although it is to abstract from whether they correspond to reality or not. So to talk of sense-impressions is to talk of nothing but the acquiring of certain beliefs. I am not claiming that this argument is conclusive, but it does have some force in supporting my thesis about sense-impressions.

6. THE ARGUMENT FROM VERIFICATION ANSWERED

We are now ready to answer the Argument from Verification. This argument starts from the premiss that our perceptions, in particular our sense-impressions, give us the *evidence*, the only evidence we have or can have, for the truth of physical-object statements. It is then inferred that physical reality cannot lie beyond the sense-impressions. And we gave the argument this much support: we agreed that if the premiss is true, the conclusion must be true also.

But we have now argued that to have a sense-impression is to acquire an 'immediate' belief or inclination to believe in some particular fact about the physical world. Now how can my belief or inclination to believe that X is Y be *evidence* for saying that X is Y? Believing that a proposition is true does nothing at all to make it true. The Argument from Verification has therefore misconstrued the relationship between sense-impressions and the physical facts. The former are the acquirings of impressions about the latter, and so cannot be evidence for them.

It might be objected here that, in some circumstances, the fact that somebody believed that X was Y could be evidence for saying that X was Y. If a person were reliable, or if he arrived at the belief by using a reliable method (for instance, by using the senses), then his *belief* that X was Y would be a good reason for believing that X *was* Y. This must be admitted, but it does not really help the Phenomenalist here. For the discovery that a certain method (say, using the senses) was a reliable method of getting *true* beliefs, would involve first discovering of the truth of beliefs of this sort *independently* of the fact that they were believed. Belief that X is Y, therefore, can only be evidence for X is Y *per accidens*. It must be based on the discovery of contingent connections holding between the way beliefs are arrived at, and the truth of these beliefs.

The special authority that we give to the reports of those who are on the spot, and whose sense-organs are working, is simply due to the fact that experience teaches us that they are in the best position to say what happened. How do we know they are in the best position to know? Perhaps we could answer this by saying that we discover it to be so in our own case. The question will then be renewed how we know *this* to be true, and the only possible answer, beside that of going round in a circle of reasons, is to say that we just *do* know. The regress of reasons must stop somewhere. It is a contingent fact about human beings and animals, a contingent fact that is so widely appreciated, and so important in our life, that it bids fair to be written into our conceptual system, that the use of the senses yields us our most reliable information about the physical world. But we can hardly give any reasons for this statement except by pointing out that it is confirmed in innumerable instances. How do we know it *is* confirmed? Well, reasons have to stop somewhere. (The Phenomenalist here is like the child who keeps *on* asking 'Why?')

Here the Phenomenalist may make a last throw. Granting that the having of sense-impressions is the acquiring of beliefs, or inclinations to believe, that something is the case in the physical

K   133

world, he can still reformulate the Argument from Verification to apply to *beliefs*. There is no intrinsic mark to distinguish true beliefs from false beliefs about the physical world. What is in fact true could have been false, what is in fact false could have been true. How then can we know which of our beliefs corresponds to reality? To say that we cannot know is to lapse into scepticism. To say, as was said above, that we just *do* know, is to lapse into dogmatism. We must therefore say that the true belief is simply the belief that *coheres best* with our other beliefs, and the beliefs of other people. We would thus reach a Phenomenalism of beliefs. The physical world would become a construction out of beliefs. Those acquirings of beliefs that we call sense-impressions would hold a central place in the construction, but only because of the contingent fact that they turned out to be the most coherent body of beliefs among all the beliefs that people have about the world. Man's beliefs would be the measure, as Protagoras held, although the individual beliefs of individuals would not necessarily be the measure, because they might fail to cohere.

This fantastic position would face all the difficulties that orthodox Phenomenalism faces, and perhaps more besides. But here all we shall argue is that a 'Phenomenalism of beliefs' cannot solve the sceptical problem with any less 'dogmatism' than the view that we have been putting forward.[1]

Coherence is a very vague notion, but let that pass. According to this 'Phenomenalism of beliefs', a belief about the physical world (e.g. that X is Y) is true if it 'coheres' with the general system of beliefs held by the believer and everybody else. That is what it means to say that X *is* Y. But how do we know that the belief that X is Y does cohere with the system in this way? The belief that X is Y has no *intrinsic* marks of coherence and incoherence, in its own nature it might be coherent or incoherent. If it is said that we just *remember* that it coheres with beliefs we have had in the past, this requires that we have a way of determining memory to be reliable. To say we cannot know that the belief coheres is to lapse into scepticism, to say we just know it does cohere is to lapse into dogmatism. To say that we should believe it coheres because the belief that it coheres, itself coheres, is to begin a vicious infinite regress. If coherence is to be used as a test, we must have a way of discovering that coherence obtains. But what

[1] My argument here owes a special debt to Professor John Anderson.

can we ever get except a *belief* that coherence obtains? And if it is said we can sometimes *know* that a certain belief coheres, then equally why not say with the Realist that we can sometimes know that a belief is true, where truth does not mean coherence?

It is no good the Phenomenalist saying that at least the other beliefs exist, and either cohere or fail to cohere with the belief that X is Y, even if, as a matter of fact, we can never establish indubitably that coherence obtains. The Realist can equally retort that the facts exist and our beliefs either succeed or fail to do justice to the facts. If the question arises what possible way we have of discovering the 'correspondence of beliefs to facts', then equally the question arises what way we have of discovering the 'coherence of our beliefs to the whole system of beliefs'.

But in any case, there is no real 'dogmatism' in claiming to know certain empirical matters of fact about the physical world, without proof. Proof must begin somewhere, so why should we not know some truths about the physical world without proof? To say that there is no intrinsic mark to distinguish true belief about the physical world from false belief, is only a way of saying that such beliefs are *contingent* and *corrigible*. It is logically possible that they should be false, and it is logically possible to be mistaken about them. But this does not show that we cannot know such truths, and know them without proof. To treat such claims to knowledge as ineluctably 'dogmatic', is to refuse to give the title of 'knowledge' to anything except necessary or incorrigible truths.

Indeed, it is only if we think of our beliefs about physical reality as *standing between ourselves and reality* that we shall find the situation in any way puzzling. We then take our beliefs about reality as our only possible *evidence* for the nature of reality, and end up by identifying reality with our coherent beliefs about it. But the problem is not solved then, for my belief that a certain belief coheres with my other beliefs will equally *stand between ourselves and the actual coherence of that belief with other beliefs*.

I conclude that, once the true nature of sense-impressions is established, the Argument from Verification collapses.

PART FOUR

The Argument from Causation

THE ARGUMENT FROM CAUSATION

LET us now pause and take stock. Common sense thinks of the physical world as a world of objects in space and time which have such qualities as colour, temperature, taste and smell (that is, all the so-called 'secondary' qualities), as well as the 'primary' qualities of shape, size, motion, etc. That is to say, common sense thinks of perception as a direct revelation of the nature of the physical world, although it does not deny that, on occasions, this revelation is obscured by error. The world is much as it looks to be, feels to be, smells to be, tastes to be, or sounds to be. At the same time the world exists quite independently of actual or possible looking, feeling, smelling, tasting or hearing.

It is this simple and straightforward view of perception and of the physical world that has come off unscathed as a result of the tedious argumentation of the last ten chapters. We have been considering, for the most part, the sort of assault on this view that was made by Berkeley, and that is still made by his descendants, the Phenomenalists. We began by examining the attempt to assimiliate some of the properties we attribute to physical objects (e.g. *heat*) to sensations. In the same chapter we examined the attempt to prove the subjectivity of some of these properties by showing that they are by nature relative. Finally we looked briefly at the attempt to assimilate these properties to sense-impressions by means of the Argument from Illusion. We saw reason to reject all these arguments. We then went on to examine a more powerful form of the Argument from Illusion which purported to show that the only direct or immediate objects of perception were our own sense-impressions. At this point we broke off to examine the *consequences* of accepting this doctrine, and we saw that it entailed some form of the Representative or the Phenomenalist theory of perception. Furthermore we discovered numerous conclusive reasons for rejecting both these doctrines. This encouraged us to re-examine this form of the Argument from Illusion; and we offered an analysis of sensory illusion which did away with the need to assume that the direct or immediate objects of perception were sense-impressions. But even this did not finally dispose of the Argument from Illusion. We found it could be revived in yet another form (which we christened the Argument from Verification), which purported to show that, since our sense-impressions are the only possible evidence for the nature of physical reality, this reality cannot lie beyond our sense-impressions. This argument we could only answer by an examination of the nature of perception itself. The examination showed that our sense-impressions are not in fact evidence for our beliefs about the physical world: they are nothing but our acquirings of immediate beliefs about that world. At this point the fury of Berkeley and the Phenomenalists seemed finally spent.

But the common-sense view of perception and of the physical world has survived these assaults only to meet with attacks from a different quarter, attacks which are as hostile to Phenomenalism as they are to Direct Realism, and which tend to reinstate some form of the Representative theory. These attacks draw their inspiration from the facts and theories of physics and physiology, and are psychologically all the more difficult to meet because of the prestige that is quite properly given to the scientific enterprise in modern thought.

There seem to be two main lines of attack here, one based on the physical and physiological mechanism of perception, the other on theories of the constitution of matter. The first we shall call the Argument from Causation (sometimes it is called the Physiological argument) and we will devote the present chapter to its consideration. The second we shall call the Argument from Science and it will occupy us in the concluding chapters of this book. We will see that this second argument leads to most serious doubts about the common-sense picture of the world that perception furnishes us with. We shall have to revise, or at any rate put into a different perspective, some of the conclusions we have already arrived at.

1. THE ARGUMENT FROM CAUSATION

The argument bases itself on the scientific discovery that, before we can perceive anything, a chain of processes must begin in the object, travel through our sense-organs, and reach the brain. (The last stages of the process are still not very clearly understood.) Until these complex processes occur, perception cannot occur. It is inferred from this that there can be no *immediate* perception of the physical object or happening that we say is perceived. The only possible *immediate* object of perception is the last link in the chain of processes. This last link is usually identified with a sense-impression, whose immediate cause is a happening in the brain.

We proceed to make a number of very familiar criticisms.

(i) If we relied on nothing but the Argument from Causation the most it would prove is that the immediate objects of perceptions are *states of our own brain*. But since we normally have no perceptual acquaintance with the things that go on inside our own skull, this is a conclusion that can hardly be accepted. It seems essential, therefore, to identify the immediate objects of perception with something that comes *later* in the causal chain than stimulation of the brain. But what does come later? The only possible candidates seem to be our *sense-impressions*. We certainly do not have sense-impressions until cortical stimulation occurs, so it seems that they must be the 'last links of the chain', that is, the immediate objects of perception.

But, of course, we then have to face the difficulty that it does not seem proper to speak of *perceiving* (and so, *a fortiori*, of *immediately* perceiving) sense-impressions. We only speak of *having* them. The only reasonable candidate for the 'last link' is therefore in danger of disqualification. And so it is here that the Argument from Causation has to turn to the Argument from Illusion for rescue. It will have to be argued that the facts of sensory illusion show that sense-impressions *are* the immediate objects of perception. But then, of course, if this can be shown independently by means of the Argument from Illusion, the Argument from Causation takes on nothing but a supporting role. And if, as we have argued, to have a sense-impression is to acquire the belief or inclination to believe that we are perceiving some physical state of affairs then it will make no sense to speak of perceiving sense-impressions. The Argument from Causation will then have to make brain-states the immediate objects of perception, which is a *reductio ad absurdum* of the argument. The only alternative would be to find some third candidate for the immediate object of perception, but there seems to be no such candidate in sight.

(ii) Critics of the Argument from Causation have regularly pointed out that, if the conclusion of the argument is true, viz. that no physical state of affairs (with the possible exception of brain-states) are ever immediately perceived, then we have no immediate evidence for the facts which are adduced as premisses of the argument, that is, the behaviour of light and sound waves, of sense-organs and of our nervous system. Their existence is just as much inferred from, or suggested by, what is immediately perceived as anything else in the physical world.

This argument seems to be a version of the familiar argument we brought against the Representative theory of perception in chapter 3, viz. that, if the theory were true, we could have no good reasons for postulating the existence of physical objects to be the causes of our immediate perceptions. Here it comes with the extra sting in its tail that, if we accepted the Representative theory on the basis of the Argument from Causation, we should have to become sceptical about the very evidence which was adduced to prove the Representative theory.

(iii) But this is but a preliminary debating point compared to the fundamental criticism that can be made of the Argument from Causation. The argument has confounded two quite distinct things: (*a*) perceiving an X or perceiving that an X is Y; and (*b*) the causal conditions which bring about this perception. It cannot be denied that perception occurs when, and only when, a certain very complex process begins in the object perceived and ends in the brain. But what warrant have we for identifying this with *perceiving*? May it not simply be the necessary, or even the necessary and sufficient, *precondition* of perception: that which must occur if perception is to occur, but which is not to be identified with perception itself? The Argument has done nothing to show that there is any identity here. And the fact that we know very well what perceiving is long before we know anything about these complex processes, suggests very strongly indeed that the two are *not* to be identified, however closely they may be related. The stick that beats me makes me jump, but my jumping is quite distinct from the stick's hitting me. The beating of the light-waves on my eyes and brain makes me see, but seeing is not identical with the beating of the light-waves.

Once we have seen this simple point we may even begin to wonder, not whether the Argument from Causation has any force, but why it ever had any persuasive power in the first place. Two reasons may be advanced.

(*a*) In the first place, it is important to emphasise once again that the Argument is making a living by taking in the dirty washing of the Argument from Illusion. We know that if our optic nerve, or our cortex, is suitably stimulated by an instrument, then we may have a perception which is indistinguishable from veridical perception, even although no physical state of affairs corresponds to the perception. It is then concluded that we have no direct perception of physical states of affairs, but only of the last links in the chain from physical object to perceiver, that is, sense-impressions. But our examination of the Argument from Illusion has shown that the facts can be dealt with in a much more satisfactory way. When our cortex is stimulated in such a fashion that we have a non-veridical perception, we should not say that there is *any* immediate object of perception involved. We should only say that this cerebral stimulation causes us to think falsely, or to be inclined to think falsely, that we are really perceiving some physical object, or state of affairs. We will simply have discovered ways of inducing false beliefs or inclinations to believe that we are perceiving. So the Argument from Causation only presents us with problems if the problems of the Argument from Illusion are unsolved. Once the latter *are* solved, the former present no independent difficulties.

(*b*) When considering the Argument from Causation, our judgement tends to be weakened by the influence of a certain model. Suppose a man holds one end of a chain in his hand, and the chain is then shaken up and down. The man may say he feels the chain moving. However, although this would be a perfectly true and proper way of speaking, it would have to be admitted that his only *immediate* tactual experience was of the movement of the link of the chain that was actually in his hand. Now it is very easy to think of the physical process from object to brain as a chain of which we can only grasp the last link in our brain or our mind. We conclude that this last link is the only immediate object of perception. But, of course, the model has only to be exhibited clearly to be rejected.

The Argument from Causation is therefore to be rejected out of hand. Only thorough-going confusion can make it in any way plausible. There is, however, one special feature of the transactions between object and perceiver that gives rise to a problem which is somewhat puzzling. We will finish the chapter by an examination of this difficulty.

2. THE ARGUMENT FROM THE TIME-GAP

It is logically possible that perception of an event should occur at exactly the same moment as the event itself occurs. Descartes actually thought that this did happen. He thought that a rod-like movement originated in the object, which produced a movement in the brain absolutely simultaneously. At the same instant that this movement in the brain occurred, the object was perceived. But we know now that in every case a time must elapse (sometimes a very short one) before a particular state of affairs is perceived. In some cases the time-gap is appreciable, when we hear distant thunder it is a few seconds, when we see the sun it is eight minutes, when we see the stars it is many years. But in every case there is *some* time-gap.

But now one may begin to wonder how we can perceive *now* what happened *then*. How can we cross the time-gap, and get to the past? The past is over and gone, and how can we see what is over and gone? Must not perception take as its object what is happening *now*? Under the influence of this line of thought one may be driven over once again to the view that the only thing that can be *immediately* perceived is something that occurs now, for example, our *present* sense-impressions. And then we have once again accepted some form of Representative theory, with all its difficulties.

A complete emancipation from this argument is not very easy, so we shall proceed by stages.

The first point to make is that, even after taking into account the speed of light and sound and of the time the brain takes to react to stimuli, there is a very good sense in which, in ordinary perception, the various events that are perceived, and the perceiving of them, all take place simultaneously.

Suppose I am looking at a number of objects in motion a few feet away from me over a period of time. Now, since the light-waves take a time to travel from the object to my eye, and impulses take a time to travel from my eye to my brain, it might seem that the objects perceived are all in the past. And if the objects are at different distances from the eye, it seems that they will be at different times in the past. But suppose now that the world were changed, so that there really was instantaneous transmission of impulses from the object perceived to the brain, as Descartes thought there was. What difference would this make to our perceptions of the same events over the same stretch of time? Surely we have every reason to believe that our perceptions would be *exactly the same*. Our perceptual apparatus is simply not sensitive enough to react differently to the tiny differences in time that would be involved, the differences would be unperceivable. To put the point in terms of sense-impressions: sense-impressions are as they appear to be, and if the times at which the impulses reached the brain were altered under an imaginary Cartesian dispensation there would be no incredibly minute differences in our sense-impressions.

But if our actual perceptions are indistinguishable from what they would be if light were propagated instantaneously, then surely it is right to say that the events we perceive, and the perceiving of them, are all happening *absolutely simultaneously*. For we would be using the phrase 'absolutely simultaneously' with the greatest precision that it *can* be used, relative to the perceptual discriminations we are able to make. It is true, of course, that there is *a* sense, a sense that would have no usefulness in ordinary talk about perception, in which there are differences in time between the various events perceived, and the perceiving of them. And it is true also that if our perceptual discriminations of time were enormously more sensitive than they actually are, then it might make a discernible perceptual difference whether light had a finite or an infinite velocity. But since the world is as it is, we are justified in saying that, in most ordinary perception, there is no time-gap to worry about.

So the cases that raise any difficulty are comparatively small in number (seeing the sun or a star, hearing distant thunder). What shall we say about these? We may begin by challenging the assumption that the time at which we perceive a certain state of affairs must be the same as the time at which that state of affairs obtains. When I 'look up at the sun', then, as the result of the stimulation of my eyes and brain by light-waves, I perceive a state of affairs that obtained on the sun eight minutes ago. It is true, of course, that, as a result of the distorting effects of the medium between the sun and myself, my perception involves a great deal of illusion. But it is certainly not totally illusory. It really is true that eight minutes ago there was a very bright hot object at a great distance from me in more or less the direction that my eyes are now pointing. My sense-impression reflects the nature of reality to that extent at least. So what we seem to have here is partially veridical perception of a state of affairs that occurred eight minutes before the perception of it occurred. *Prima acie*, this falsifies the contention that we can only perceive what is going on *now*. And if we accept the thesis that perception is the acquiring of knowledge of, or inclination to believe in, particular facts about the world by means of our senses, it seems that there can be no objection to saying that, when we 'look at the sun', we acquire some knowledge of what was happening in a distant portion of space eight minutes ago. Since the distance is so great, it is not surprising that the knowledge acquired is meagre, and that a large element of false belief or inclination to false belief is involved.

We may now be inclined to say that it is a mere contingent fact that most of the happenings that we perceive happen at the same time as our perception of them. For could we not conceive of a world where the processes that lead up to perception occur so slowly that this is not true? Consider the following experiment. An equilateral triangle with sides of half a mile is marked out, and I stand at one corner. Another observer stands at another corner, and it is arranged that some striking visual phenomenon should occur at the third corner (for example, the igniting of a piece of magnesium). The second observer is instructed to give a signal the moment he sees the flare, while I keep watch both for the flare and the observer's signal. Now, in this situation, it is an empirical fact that I will perceive the flare and the signal at about the same instant. This is incompatible with the assumption that the considerable distance involves a considerable time-gap between the event perceived and the perception of it. For if light took, say, a minute to travel half a mile, I would see the observer's signal a full minute after I saw the flare.

Now, it may be argued, experiments of this sort merely show us in a strict and formal way what ordinary experience shows us in a loose and informal way. It seems, therefore, that there is no necessity for the time of the event perceived to be the same as the time of the perception of it. It is simply a very familiar fact which we discover by experience to be normally the case. (If it were not normally the case, perception would be much less useful in the conduct of life.)

However, we have been slurring over a most important point. If we confine ourselves to what seems to be *immediately* perceived, that is, if we confine ourselves to our sense-impressions, we must admit that our impression is always of something that exists *in the present*.

If an astronomer sees a star vanish, there is no doubt that he perceives the past. And he may perceive it *as past*. But his sense-impressions are impressions of something happening now: a light seems to go out in the sky now. If our analysis of perception is correct, he will have an inclination to believe falsely that something is happening up above him in the sky now. His immediate perception involves *illusion* about time, even if about nothing else, and it is only his mediate perception that is veridical.[1] So it seems that we cannot have immediate perception of the past *as past*. Our immediate perception of past happenings must involve illusion, illusion about the time of the happening immediately perceived.

In the case of the star, it may be questioned whether our immediate perception really involves any temporal illusion. It may be suggested that what we immediately perceive is not the star, but a *present* happening, causally connected with the extinction of the star many years ago. The star sends a message to us, as it were, and we immediately perceive the *message*, not the star. Now this suggestion may be correct in the case of *sound*.[2] There seems to be some force in thinking of sound as actually spreading out from its source, like a balloon rapidly inflating. (And here I am not

---

[1] It is a curious situation when immediate perceptual *illusion* gives us mediate *knowledge* of the world, but it is a perfectly familiar one. The same thing occurs in the case of mirror-images.

[2] This was pointed out to me by Dr. A. C. Jackson.

speaking of the sound-*waves*.) So when two people 'hear the same sound' it may be argued with some plausibility that they *immediately* hear two different things, because they are in different positions.

These considerations may dissolve the problem of the time-gap when we hear a 'distant' sound. But the suggestion seems inapplicable to the case of the star. What could the immediate objects of sight be? They could not be our sense-impressions, for we cannot perceive sense-impressions. They could not be the light-waves from the star, for we do not see light-waves. The only possible immediate object of sight is *the star itself*. But then we must admit that our perception involves temporal illusion, because the star's extinction appears to be occurring *now*.

So it seems that immediate perception is sometimes a perception of past happenings. But, at the same time, the past cannot be immediately perceived *as past*. All perception of the past as past is mediate perception. There is no *perception* of a time-gap in immediate perception.

Ironically, however, this *absence* of a time-gap in immediate perception gives rise to two serious problems.

(i) We must admit that the notion of perceptual illusion is co-ordinate with the notion of veridical perception. When we speak of immediate perceptual illusion, it should at least make sense to speak of immediately perceiving the true state of affairs. When I press my eye-ball, the candle-flame looks double. But it is possible for the candle-flame to look as it is. Now suppose that when somebody perceives a star vanish, he simultaneously perceives the flight of a bird. It looks to him as if a bright object vanishes from the sky at the same instant as a thing with a bird-like shape moves across the sky. But, in fact, the first event occurred long before the second event, and so immediate perceptual illusion is involved. But if the concept of immediate perceptual illusion is co-ordinate with the concept of immediate veridical perception, it seems that it should at least *make sense* to speak of immediately perceiving the true state of affairs. We should be able to perceive immediately that the first event occurred long before the second event. But the difficulty is that we cannot understand what it would be like to perceive this. I can understand having the immediate perception that the bright thing in the sky is *very much further away* from my body than the object with the bird-like shape. (Of course, immediate perception only gives me 'very much further away'.) But what would it be like to perceive immediately that the extinction of the light occurred *very much before* the motion of the bird-like object? This is far from clear.

(ii) We have put forward the view that immediate perception is nothing but the acquiring of immediate knowledge of, or inclination to believe in, facts about the physical world, by means of the senses. Now, if this is so, it seems that immediate perception of the past should be logically possible. Why should I not acquire immediate information about the past, knowing it to be the past, by using my senses? If we cannot give sense to the notion of immediate perception of the past as past, it seems that our account of perception may be in jeopardy. Yet it is not clear what immediate perception of the past as past would be like.

We shall first notice two unsuccessful attempts to evade these problems, and then propose our own solution.

It might be said that it is quite easy to imagine immediately perceiving that the extinction of the star occurred years before the motion of the bird. Suppose that the velocity of light was infinite, and my span of attention indefinitely long. At a certain time I perceive a light go out in the sky. I keep my eyes fixed on the sky for some years, and am finally rewarded by seeing a bird-like shape. I have perceived that the first happening preceded the second.

But this answer is unsatisfactory. Why is it impossible to perceive a time-gap of years, except by taking years to do it? In order to perceive a great distance, I do not have to traverse the distance. In order to hear a sound, I do not have to be making that sound itself. Why, then, must it take years to perceive a time-gap of years? Why cannot we perceive the gap instantaneously?

It might be objected here, that if immediate perception of the past as past were to occur, it would not *be* perception, but would be memory. However, this objection is incorrect. For it is essential to the notion of remembering something that what we remember should have been perceived or learnt before. Memory-knowledge (whether memory of events or of anything else), is previously acquired knowledge. Now the case we want is one where we acquire immediate knowledge of the past, known as the past, without any previous perception.

In order to solve the difficulty, let us consider our immediate perception of *succession*. Suppose that a green light shines for a brief time, and then goes out. At the same instant that it goes out, a red light is turned on. It also shines for a brief time, to be succeeded by the green light again, and so on. We could find a minimum time for which each light would have to shine, while still permitting a certain observer to pick out every step in the cycle. We may imagine that the lights are shone for just this minimum time, and no longer.

Suppose now that the observer watches the cycle of lights for one minute. He sees a succession of events that lasts for one minute. Presumably we would also say that his *seeing* of these events lasted a minute. But now let us consider what it is that the observer immediately perceives at a particular instant. We take 'instant' here to mean not 'mathematical instant', but a duration only just sufficient to permit the observer to see whichever light is shining. Can we say of the observer *at that instant* that he immediately perceives anything but the light that is shining *at that instant*? I do not think we can, because the events that occurred previously have already been perceived at previous instants. It follows that they cannot be said to be perceived *at that instant*, but only to be remembered. If we talk about immediate perception at an instant, confining ourselves to ordinary contexts where the object perceived is at no great spatial distance, the only thing immediately perceived in that instant is the state of affairs at that instant.

Now the great difficulty that is often felt about this argument is that, if it were valid, we would never have any immediate perception of succession, but only a succession of perceptions. For consider our perception of any event that involves a distinguishable succession of phases. If we can distinguish successive phases, then it seems that our perceptions of these successive phases will occur at successive instants. But, if this is so, our perception of the earlier phase will be over by the time that the later phase is perceived, and so the first phase will not be perceived, but only remembered. How, then, are we to *perceive* the succession of phases?[1] It seems that all we have is a succession of perceptions.

Despite its attractiveness, however, I think this objection is invalid. When I immediately perceive a certain state of affairs at

[1] In Kantian terms, how is the synthesis of reproduction possible?

a certain instant (for instance, that the green light is on), I do not immediately perceive what has been happening in previous instants. At the present instant, what *has* happened is remembered, not perceived. But why cannot I immediately perceive now that the state of affairs that obtains now *has succeeded to* the previous states of affairs? There seems to be no reason why I should not immediately perceive this *without now perceiving those previous states of affairs*. After all, the present state of affairs has succeeded to whatever was the previous state of affairs. Why should I not acquire this immediate information by the use of my senses, yet not be now perceiving that previous state of affairs?

Our difficulty in accepting this seems to lie in our desire to make the immediate object of perception something substantial. (It is this desire, of course, that leads to the doctrine that the immediate objects of perception are sense-impressions or sense-data.) In the present case, the immediate object of perception is 'that this present state of affairs has succeeded to previous states of affairs'. But we crave something more solid than this for the immediate object of perception: we crave an *object* which shall exhibit successive phases. And so we demand that, if we are ever to perceive succession immediately, the previous state of affairs be perceived along with the present state of affairs, all in the same instant. But, as we have seen, we are then faced with the difficulty that the previous state of affairs has already been perceived, and so is not perceived now, but only remembered.

We are now in a position to solve the problem about the star. We have seen that in ordinary cases of immediate perception, in the paradigm cases where the objects we perceive are at no great spatial distance, the events perceived occur at the same time as the perception of them. An event that occurred in the past would have been perceived in the past, and so could only be remembered now. I suggest that this fact tends to be written into the concept of immediate perception. We tend to make it a logical necessity that what I now immediately perceive must exist now. There is a contingent fact involved, a fact about the speed of reaction of our sensory apparatus to physical events in our environment; but a conceptual necessity about immediate perception is erected on the foundation of this contingent fact. The discovery that we see the stars as they were many years ago comes as something of a shock to our conceptual system. But it does not force any *extensive* conceptual revision on us, for, when we look at the stars with this new knowledge, it still *looks* as if we are immediately perceiving present events. We need only say that what I immediately perceive now must at least *seem* to exist now.

So to talk about looking into the sky, and acquiring, by the use of the senses, immediate information that something had happened in the past, would be a case for which we have no linguistic rules ready. We could not call it memory, for memory entails previous perception. We could not call it mediate perception, for that would be contrary to the description of the case as the *immediate* acquiring of information. We could not call it immediate perception, for we want to say that what is immediately perceived at least appears to exist in the present. We can certainly imagine that, by use of our senses, we should immediately acquire knowledge about the past, known as being past. We can imagine this knowledge being of the same sort as our perceptual knowledge, and just as detailed. But we should be reluctant to call it *perception*, although we would have no other single term to label it by. There is, of course, an excellent reason for this: this sort of phenomenon does not in fact occur. It is a mere logical possibility, for which our language has not provided.

Our argument has been complex and difficult, and in such a case error is only too easy. But it may be hoped that we have now elucidated the main problems posed by the Argument from the Time-gap, and have shown that the facts involve no threat to our Direct Realism or to our analysis of perception. We have seen that, paradoxically enough, the trickiest problems are raised, not by the presence of a time-gap in perception, but by its *absence* in immediate perception.

PART FIVE

The Argument from Science

12

THE ARGUMENT FROM
SCIENCE

WE have now to face the last of the great assaults on the Direct
Realist account of perception, the argument or arguments
drawn from the modern scientific account of the constitution of
matter. I should explain at the outset that I feel greatly
handicapped by my considerable ignorance of scientific matters.
But the arguments are too important to evade; if we do not
discuss them a great gap has been left in our account of perception.

Like the Argument from Causation (and quite unlike the Argument from Illusion), the Argument from Science can be stated
very briefly. Modern physics gives an account of the nature of
matter which seems to be completely at variance with the deliverances of perception. According to physics, ordinary material
objects are collections of enormously minute particles called
molecules, each different sort of material substance being made up
of different sorts of molecules. Molecules, in turn, are composed
of still smaller particles called *atoms*, each different sort of atom
being the smallest possible particle of a particular *element*. The
constitution of the atom is still being investigated. When the atom
was first shown to be further divisible, it was thought to be composed of two sorts of particles only, *electrons* and *protons*. But later
research has discovered a bewildering variety of 'fundamental
particles'. These particles are credited with such properties as
mass, electric charge, velocity, spin and position. It is in some
degree doubtful, however, whether these 'fundamental particles'

should be treated as being particles, because in some respects they behave like *waves*.

Now this account of the nature of matter is certainly not put forward by physicists as a complete one. It may have to be added to, refined, or even altered, by subsequent research. But if this account, or anything like it, is true, then it seems that the world that perception gives us is a mere sham. Colour, sound, taste and smell, for instance, play no part in the physicist's account of matter, although perception treats them as characteristics of physical objects. Physical objects look and feel solid, 'what is standing close to what is' as Parmenides puts it, but, if the physicist's account is correct, they are mostly empty space ('fundamental particles' can be shot straight through them). Nothing is as it seems to be.

Faced with this situation it is very natural to solve the problem by adopting a Representative theory of perception, treating the 'perceptual world' as a mere series of sense-impressions caused in the mind by physical reality. This sort of approach is exemplified by Eddington when he says colour is mere 'mind-spinning'. But, however natural is the attempt to escape the discrepancy between the two descriptions of reality in this way, we have seen that to adopt a Representative theory leads to insoluble problems. We want to find some solution to the problem within the limits of a Direct Realist theory of perception.

I. SCIENTIFIC PHENOMENALISM

Now there is a very well-known line of solution to this difficulty which was adumbrated by Berkeley and worked out in more detail by Mach and others. We may call it a 'Phenomenalism of scientific entities', but we must distinguish it carefully from Phenomenalism about physical objects, the attempt to give an account of physical objects purely in terms of sense-impressions, which we have called simply 'Phenomenalism'. This approach to the problem is exemplified in Berkeley's discussion of the concepts of *force*, *gravity* and *attraction*. We are not to think, he says, that when we talk about these things we are speaking of any occult entities distinct from the phenomena. We are simply putting forward a scheme for the systematic description of the actual observed motions of things, and are also predicting the further course of such motions.[1] Berkeley is arguing that these concepts are all, in the modern phrase, *theoretical concepts*, concepts which offer a description of observed phenomena, and prediction of phenomena to come, but which do not involve postulating the existence of anything beyond the phenomena. Now this account of the concepts of force, gravity and attraction is hardly a matter of controversy now. It would be quite generally accepted. But it gives us a model for understanding how a 'Phenomenalism of scientific entities' would deal with such things as molecules, atoms, protons and electrons. They, too, would be said to be theoretical concepts, simply classifying the observed phenomena and predicting the results of further observations.

This treatment of scientific entities is inevitable for Phenomenalists about physical objects, who want to give an account of the whole physical world in terms of sense-impressions. Indeed we might characterise a Phenomenalism of physical objects by saying that it tries (most implausibly) to construe the concept of a physical object as if it were a theoretical concept, a conceptual device for organising and predicting the flow of our sense-impressions. Once we hold such a doctrine of the nature of physical objects, it is inevitable that we should go on to give an account of *all* the concepts of physical science in terms of sense-impressions.

So a Phenomenalism of material objects *entails* a Phenomenalism of scientific entities. *But the reverse entailment does not hold.* A Realist could quite well accept a Phenomenalism of scientific entities, but go on to say that the 'phenomena' which were to be organised, and whose behaviour was to be predicted, were not sense-impressions but *physical objects* or *physical events*.

So perhaps the Direct Realist can evade the conclusions of the Argument from Science by arguing that these entities of which the physicist speaks, molecules, atoms, electrons, protons, light-waves, etc., are simply *theoretical concepts*. Perhaps talk about such entities is an extremely complex and sophisticated way of attempting to organise our observations of the behaviour of ordinary

---

[1] Cf. especially *De Motu* sec. 17. '*Force, gravity, attraction*, and terms of this sort are useful for reasonings and reckonings about motion and bodies in motion, but not for understanding the simple nature of motion itself or for indicating so many distinct qualities.' Translated by A. A. Luce. *Collected Works*, vol. 4.

physical objects in certain situations. The use of these concepts might quite regularly be associated with certain *models* or *pictures*, which might be extremely misleading if taken as a literal guide to the nature of physical reality, but which might be very useful, might even be psychologically essential, *within the context of the theory*. The exact connection of the theories embodied in these concepts with the observable behaviour of physical objects may be incredibly complex, providing indefinite work for the new discipline of the Philosophy of Science. But as Wittgenstein said:

> Through their whole logical apparatus the physical laws still speak of the objects of the world. (Tractatus, 6.3431.)

And the Realist may interpret 'the world' as the world disclosed by perception, the world of ordinary physical objects.

Nor need the fact that the physicist makes certain *omissions* in his account of nature, dismissing as mere 'secondary qualities' such characteristics of physical objects as colour, sound, taste, smell, etc., be any bar to this 'Phenomenalism of scientific entities'. The fact that the physicist only mentions certain characteristics of physical objects such as length, mass, motion, shape, etc., implies only that he is *selecting* certain characteristics of objects for his attention. Perhaps he is selecting those characteristics which play a specially important role in the causal order of nature (a ball obeys exactly the same laws of motion whatever colour or smell it may have), without in any way derogating from the objective reality of the other characteristics.

In some such way as this, then, we may attempt to come to terms with the Argument from Science without in any way departing from a Direct Realist theory of perception or a common-sense view of the nature of the objects perceived.

2. DIFFICULTIES FOR SCIENTIFIC PHENOMENALISM

Now I have a great deal of sympathy for this view (although lacking the detailed knowledge that would be necessary to work it out fully), and would not want to rule it out completely. It might be the true view. And even if we cannot treat *everything* in the physicist's account of the nature of reality in this way, it is still a most valuable conception to use when considering some *parts* of physical theory (such concepts as gravitation cry out for such treatment). The substituting of logical constructions for inferred entities seems to me, as it seemed to Russell, to be the path of virtue.

Even when this method fails, we still must not despair of reconciling physics and perception. It is perfectly possible that the physicist should discover indirect evidence for the existence of entities which are never immediately perceived, but which exist along with the objects discovered by perception. There is nothing in Direct Realism to show that the catalogue of the immediate objects of perception *exhausts* the nature of reality. We have good reasons for believing that there are many things which *as a matter of fact* we are completely unable to perceive, and whose existence we can only discover by their perceived effects. Now it may be possible to give such an account of some of the scientific entities discovered by physics.

Nevertheless, there seem to be a number of points of scientific detail which suggest that the physicist's account of the nature of things does not merely give us a more comprehensive and detailed view of reality than ordinary perception does, but actually *clashes* with the latter at a number of points. These observations may be divided into two classes: (i) observations which seem to support a *Realistic* as opposed to a *Phenomenalistic* account of molecules, atoms and the 'fundamental particles', (ii) observations which seem to cast doubt on the objectivity of the 'secondary qualities', in particular *colour*. These observations must now be discussed briefly.

A number of these disturbing observations are made with *microscopes*. Such observations have great authority with us, and it is worth while to consider first why this should be so. Consider what it is that happens when we look at an object through a low-power magnifying-glass. In one way the magnifying-glass produces a visual illusion, because it makes the object look to be larger than it is. (Imagine one was looking at the object with one naked eye, while the glass was in front of the other eye.) But in other ways the magnifying-glass does not distort, but reveal. Suppose we were looking at some marks on a stamp which we could perceive with the naked eye, but only with the greatest difficulty. The magnifying-glass would show us the marks clearly and distinctly, perhaps also showing us more detail than we could make out with the naked eye. But we would trust these new deliverances because we had been able to check the glass against the naked eye to some extent. We could then substitute a more powerful glass, checking *its* reliability by reference back to the original glass; and so proceed by easy stages to the most powerful microscope.

This is why, when a line that looks absolutely straight to the naked eye looks jagged under the microscope, we trust the microscope rather than the eye. Berkeley says that a microscope 'takes us, as it were, into a new world'.[1] But the Realist, at least, thinks of it as yielding detailed and precise information about small portions of the objects in *this* world. The line really is jagged, even although the indentations are very small indeed. We are able to see these small indentations with a microscope although we could not see them with the naked eye. The only element of illusion involved is that it looks to us as if we are seeing an ordinary jagged line, that is, a line of ordinary size with quite large indentations. But this we discount as illusion. In everything else, however, we side with the microscope as being more reliable than the naked eye.

Now, the revelation that a line that looks absolutely straight to the naked eye is very often full of tiny indentations leads us to no very startling revision of the common-sense view of the world. It only shows that ordinary perception is rather rough-and-ready in such matters, which is not a very surprising conclusion. But some of the other things revealed by microscopes are much more troubling.

Consider a given quantity of standing water. It looks to be continuous and uniform, and its constituent parts appear to be at rest. Now if we take the molecular theory *literally* the water consists of an enormous number of discrete water-molecules, all in very violent random motion. The phenomenalist about scientific entities would have to say that, for the purposes of predicting the results of certain experiments, it is convenient to treat the water *as if* this description were true of it, although ordinary observation manifestly shows us that it is not true.

But if lycopodium particles are suspended in the water, and are then observed under a suitable microscope, they will be seen to behave just as if they are being bombarded by particles in violent motion (although, admittedly, the particles that are doing the

---

[1] *New Theory of Vision*, sec. 85.

bombardment are not seen). This phenomenon, called Brownian movement, Einstein showed to be just that which one would expect if there were particles doing the bombardment having the properties of molecules of water. It is true that the Phenomenalist can still say that the lycopodium particles simply behave *as if* they were being bombarded by minute particles. But it seems much more natural to suppose that the bombardment is a real one.

In recent times the very powerful *electron microscope* has provided even more convincing evidence against a Phenomenalism about molecules. Photographs have been obtained of large molecules, and the photographs confirm the predictions about the shape, size and arrangement of parts of these molecules which were reached from purely theoretical considerations. The Phenomenalist about molecules can still point out that our perception of the molecules is not *immediate* (as it is when we look down a microscope barrel at something), but is mediated by perception of another physical object, viz. a photographic plate. He *could* then argue that the patterns that appear on the plate are not literal pictures of physical reality. Yet this hardly seems very plausible. Similar difficulties for a Phenomenalist account of the 'fundamental particles' are raised by the photographs of the 'tracks' of particles in the Wilson cloud chamber.

Such observations push one very violently towards a Realistic interpretation of the physicist's theories of matter. At the same time there is some evidence that seems to cast doubt on the objective reality of colour, and so, by implication, the other qualities that are omitted from the physicist's account of the physical world. If coloured surfaces are scrutinised under the microscope, the apparent colours of the portion of the surface observed are quite different from, and incompatible with, the colours the surfaces seem to have for normal observers under standard conditions. To ordinary vision blood looks to be red through and through. But under a microscope a quite different pattern is revealed: it does not seem to be everywhere red. Different magnifications yield different, incompatible, colour-appearances. The question then arises what we are to say is the real colour of the surface. There seems no reason to favour the appearance presented to the normal observer under standard conditions. If we all had microscopic eyes, the normal observer would give us a quite different report. If we say we should trust the most powerful microscope available, we shall have to keep changing our view of the matter with every advance in technique. Since the physicists have no theory about the *real* colour of a certain surface (as opposed to its *real* structure), it is therefore tempting to say that colour is mere subjective illusion at all times. And once we say this of colour, it seems we must say the same of sound, taste, smell, and perhaps heat and cold, all the qualities that the physicist ignores.

It might be suggested here that there is no difficulty in saying that a drop of blood is *really* red, or, at any rate, portions of a drop of blood are really red, and yet also saying that *very minute* portions have a different colour, or have no colour at all. A man is rational, but his hand is not rational. Why could not the same be true of the redness of drops of blood?

But although the parts of a (rational) man are not rational, the (coloured) parts of a coloured thing or coloured surface must be coloured all over.[1] Now it is a perfectly intelligible suggestion that objects or surfaces of a certain colour should have a fixed minimum size. Colour would then be an 'emergent' property of objects, a property only found in physical objects of a certain size and structure. But in such a case it still seems that either the object or its surface would be coloured all over, or else proper parts would be coloured all over. Just because the thing would lose colour once its parts disintegrated, we cannot say that, while the parts are together, it is not they that are coloured. The situation is quite different from the rationality of a man. The truth of this may be concealed when we think of the minimum size of a coloured object as a very small size. But it is an equally intelligible, although false, suggestion that the minimum size for a red surface should be a foot square. Yet it would be quite unintelligible to say that, although the whole surface was red, no proper part of the surface was red. It is equally unintelligible, I think, to say that there is a very small minimum size for coloured things or surfaces, and add that the parts of a thing or surface of minimum size are not coloured.

So if a drop of blood really is red, then it is red *all over*, or proper parts of the drop are red *all over*. These parts cannot simul-

---

[1] In the terms that Aristotle applied to his 'substances', a rational thing is, qua rational, an anomoeomerous thing, while a coloured thing or surface is, qua coloured, an homoeomerous thing.

taneously be another colour, or be colourless. So the new colours, or lack of colour, revealed when a drop of blood is scrutinised under a microscope, are actually *incompatible* with the appearance presented to the naked eye. There is a conflict of appearances here, and at least one of the colour-perceptions *must* involve illusion. Once this is admitted, it is tempting to say that all colour-perception is a subjective illusion. For there seems no way to decide the *real* colour.

A further argument against the objective reality of colours is provided by the great complexity of the correlations between the intensity and wave-length of the light emitted by the surface, and the colour presented to the observer. All sorts of different combinations of intensity and wave-length may produce the same colour-perception.[1] Colours therefore seem to 'fit on' to the features of the world recognised by physics in a very untidy way. If we are already inclined to take a realistic view of scientific entities, it will be no easy matter to correlate the properties of these objects with colours. The correlation will lack any real ground or connection with the rest of physical theory.

None of these considerations is *decisive*, but they do indicate the strength of the case for a realistic account of at least some portions of microphysics; an account which will clash with the deliverances of ordinary perception.

Let us therefore grant, for the sake of argument, that the physicist's account of reality is more or less on the right track (though inevitably incomplete and perhaps in some degree erroneous). Must we then retreat into a Representative theory of perception? Is a Realistic account of scientific entities incompatible with a Direct Realist theory of perception? Now, in defending Direct Realism against the Argument from Illusion in chapter 7, we gave an account of sensory illusion as being a false belief, or inclination to believe, that we are perceiving some real feature of the physical world. (In a later chapter we went on to give an analysis of perception itself which permitted a deeper appreciation of the nature of sensory illusion. But this further analysis need not be appealed to here.) Now perhaps the Direct

---

[1] This argument was put to me by Professor J. J. C. Smart. It would only be strengthened if the new theory of colour recently proposed by E. H. Land is correct. Cf. 'Experiments in Colour Vision', *Scientific American*, vol. 200, no. 5 (May 1959).

Realist could accept the physicist's account of the nature of physical reality (as far as it goes), but retain Direct Realism by saying that what the physicist has shown is *that sensory illusion is a much more widespread affair than we ordinarily assume.* We should have to say that, not just what we ordinarily take to be illusory perceptions, but even what we ordinarily take to be *veridical* perceptions, are in fact deeply infected by error, that is, involve a great deal of sensory illusion.[1] In this way we could reconcile Direct Realism with the physicist's account of reality, without having to embrace a complete 'Phenomenalism of scientific entities'.

So in the last three chapters of this book I want to work out this suggestion in detail. I shall try to do this by considering the objections that might be brought against such a view. We shall see that it involves real problems, which make it difficult to see how the physicist's picture can be a complete description of reality. But something very close to the physicist's conception of reality may emerge as a plausible account of the actual nature of the physical world.

[1] We have already seen that the Representative theory was correct in asserting (i) that in veridical perception, the perception is caused by the object perceived (chap. 10, sec. 2); (ii) that our sense-impressions correspond or fail to correspond to reality (chap. 10, sec. 5. (vi)). Now we must recognize a third insight of this theory: (iii) physical reality may radically fail to correspond to what common sense calls veridical perception. The only error of the Representative theory was to place sense-impressions between us and physical reality. We have avoided this by taking sense-impressions to *be* our apprehensions of physical reality.

13

DIRECT REALISM
WITHOUT SCIENTIFIC
PHENOMENALISM

WE are now assuming that the physicist's account of reality is a literal picture of the physical world (subject of course to the modifications and corrections the physicist may want to make as a result of further discoveries). The discrepancy between the physicist's account of reality and the deliverances of perception is accounted for by saying that ordinary perception involves sensory illusion to a greater degree than common-sense allows. For since, as we agreed in chapter 7,[1] an account can be given of sensory illusion without having to accept either a Representative or a Phenomenalist theory, there is no falling away from Direct Realism in thus extending the range of sensory illusion. We shall now consider possible objections to this thesis. We need not confine ourselves here to objections that might be brought by somebody who was arguing against Direct Realism by means of the Argument from Science, but may consider any arguments that seem powerful, whatever their antecedents.

[1] We shall not *need* to appeal to the deeper analysis of sensory illusion proposed in chapter 9. As this account is the more controversial, and as it does not *contradict* the analysis proposed in chapter 7, it will be exposing less flank if we do not appeal to it.

1. CAN SCIENTIFIC FINDINGS UNDERMINE PERCEPTION?

It is clear that science is based on observation, on the use of our senses. If physics ends up by rejecting the senses, it seems to be fouling its own nest, assaulting its own method of reaching truth. A Scientific Phenomenalism would avoid this paradox, and may therefore seem to be preferable.

Now I think it must be admitted that it would be a quite intolerable position if our view of the physical world clashed with our perceptions *at all points*. We have, as a matter of fact, no other reliable means of discovering the nature of the physical world except by the use of our senses. If our theories about the nature of the physical world cannot be established by our perceptions, they cannot be established at all. But it may be doubted whether this prevents us from embracing a physical theory which allows a very wide divergence between the theory, and a great many features of ordinary perceptions.

The first demand that we must make on a physical theory which claims to discover the existence of objects or properties of objects that are not perceived by the senses, is that these objects or properties of objects must be *in principle* immediately perceivable, even if, by hypothesis, they are never immediately perceived. This demand is not as harsh as it may sound. Modern physics claims that certain features of its 'fundamental particles' are imperceptible in principle. But all that is meant is that, *if a particular theory of the physical world is true*, certain observations of the particle's properties can never be made. But all that I am claiming is that it must not be *logically impossible* for the objects or properties of objects postulated to be perceived immediately. There is nothing in physical theory to bar this demand. Visual perception takes place by means of light, and the properties of light therefore set a limit to certain sorts of observation. But we can well *imagine* visual perception which was not tied to the properties of light in this way, thus permitting immediate visual perception of certain states of affairs that modern physics quite rightly treats as unobservable.

The second demand that we must make on a physical theory is that it be actually testable by ordinary observation. Observations must be possible which will confirm or disconfirm it. But this does not imply that the theory itself need be based upon, or even

suggested by, observation. (Kepler's faith that there were comparatively simple laws of planetary motion was in no way suggested by observation.) Nor does it mean that such a theory
cannot discount as illusory much of our ordinary observation.
All that is needed is that *certain* observations should be veridical
or involve veridical elements (for example, the observation that a
certain pointer is at a certain position on a scale, even if the
pointer and the scale are not in reality as they seem to the senses
to be). If such observations strikingly favour the theory this may
be a good reason for accepting it, even if it involves treating
many of our other observations as more or less illusory. In a
completely worked out view of the world, of course, a full
scientific explanation would have to be given of such sensory
illusion. But there seems to be no reason why this should not
be done within the framework of the physicist's conception of
reality.

There is, then, nothing self-refuting in using selected deliverances of the senses to overthrow the other deliverances. A theory
that demands such widespread condemnation of ordinary observation must, of course, be tested by its fruits. But if they are forthcoming, it seems that there is no objection to accepting the
theory. We would not be sawing off the branch we were sitting on,
but sitting on a branch and sawing off the outermost part, the
part on which we were *not* sitting. Provided we left ourselves
room on the branch, this would be a perfectly safe procedure.

2. THE ARGUMENT FROM PARADIGM CASES

We say that a drop of blood not merely looks to be, but
actually *is*, red all over. We contrast it with a drop of water, which
we say is not red. We say that a table not merely looks to have,
but actually does have, a continuous surface. We contrast it with
a sieve, which we say does not have a continuous surface. These
are *paradigm* cases of objects that we say are red all over, or that
have a continuous surface: the sort of objects that we would use
to teach a child the use of the corresponding phrases. The
linguistic conventions that govern the uses of the phrases 'red all
over' and 'continuous surface' are set up by reference to objects
such as drops of blood and tables. The child is taught to apply
these phrases to drops of blood and to tables, and to deny the

THE ARGUMENT FROM SCIENCE

phrases to drops of water or sieves. It is quite possible, of course, that the teaching will proceed by reference to other objects than these. But, at any rate, they are *among* the objects that would be appropriate for such teaching.

Now, if this is so, it may be argued that it is nonsense to deny that drops of blood are red all over, or that tables have a continuous surface. To make such a denial is simply *to attempt to repudiate a linguistic convention*. It is to refuse to apply words in the way that they are applied by the world at large.

But despite the popularity and influence of this sort of argument in modern philosophy, I cannot find it very convincing. It should surely be obvious that we apply descriptions to physical objects in virtue of our perceptions of these objects. I am not asserting that our perceptions of objects are full and entire before we come to talk about them. No doubt our language is not cut off from perception with a hatchet. The way we talk about the world modifies the way we perceive it. But, *in general*, language follows perception, we can perceive before we can speak or understand speech. It follows from this that we apply ordinary descriptions to ordinary objects in virtue of our perceptual classifications. Our senses suggest to us resemblances and differences between things; and these are the basis for the way we talk about things. Objects' natures do not lie transparently open to us, these natures have to be discovered by the use of the senses.

Now, since we have utterly rejected Phenomenalism, we must surely admit that our perceptions may more or less radically fail to reflect reality; that they may involve us in a misclassification of objects, of the classing together of things as similar in respects in which they are not similar. And so our ordinary descriptions of objects, normally following rather than creating our perceptions, will reflect our perceptual errors. Ordinary descriptions of ordinary objects, therefore, may well have error written into the descriptions, may presuppose that the objects have a certain nature which in fact they do not have.[1] It may presuppose that

---

[1] We may concede Wittgenstein the point that:

'If language is to be a means of communication there must be agreement not only in definitions but also . . . in judgements.' (*Investigations*, sec. 242.)

But notice that Wittgenstein only speaks of *agreements* in judgements, and not that the judgements that are agreed upon must be *true*.

drops of blood are everywhere similar in colour, or that the surface of a table is absolutely continuous.

It is true, of course, as we admitted in the previous section, that the nature of man is such that he has nothing except perception to discover the errors of perception. This means that we cannot repudiate perception as entirely erroneous. Indeed, to say that physics shows that my table has a quite different nature from the nature it seems to reveal to our senses, presupposes that we can still go on talking about the *table*. This in turn presupposes that there are some identifying features *common* to the descriptions of physics and common sense (e.g. 'the thing that is at a certain place at a certain time'). And this implies that we have not repudiated perception *entirely*. But, granting this, it still seems that it is perfectly meaningful to say that ordinary perception may be deeply infected with error, even in those situations which we ordinarily regard as paradigm cases of perceiving that a certain thing really has a certain property. In teaching a child to describe certain objects in a certain way, we may be simply teaching him to apply the same word as ourselves in virtue of certain tendencies to classify that we and the child have in common. But these classifications may still falsify the nature of reality.

But at this point it will be objected that, if people have the perceptual reactions to physical objects that they do have, and if they mark their discriminations of certain resemblances and differences by certain words, then, if this really is the way they use the words, this is the correct usage. It cannot be impugned by any theory that our perceptions fail to correspond to physical reality in many respects.

I now want to suggest that this argument is correct in a way. What it shows is that, despite all the criticisms we have made of Phenomenalism, it does have a *limited* truth, although this truth does nothing to contradict the truth of Direct Realism.

I think we must now admit, in the face of the objection just mentioned, that there is a perfectly good 'pragmatic' sense in which a drop of blood *really* is red (as opposed to a drop of water), and a table *really* does have a continuous surface (as opposed to a sieve). And the meaning of 'really is' here is simply 'presents that appearance to normal observers under standard conditions'. In ordinary life we require the distinction between normal and abnormal perception for all sorts of purposes, and it would be churlish in a philosopher (as well as impossible) to stop people using such phrases as 'really is' and 'is not really' to make the contrast.

What happens is that we *begin* by thinking that the appearances that objects present to normal observers under standard conditions are the *real* properties of objects. That is to say, we think that the appearances correspond to physical reality. Later, the physicist convinces us that this is not so. The physicist forces us to change our view of the *denotation* of the word 'real' when applied to our perceptions, because we want to preserve the *connotation*. But what are we to say about the appearances that we previously accounted veridical? We still want to distinguish the appearances presented to normal observers under standard conditions from other appearances. In any case, it is very natural, after we have applied a certain description to a certain range of objects, to go on doing so even when we have cause to think that the description is misapplied. The description clings to what once seemed to be its denotation, and will not be easily detached. So we invent a *second* sense of 'real' as applied to perceptions. In this second sense, it is *tautological* to say that the appearances that objects present to normal observers under standard conditions are the real properties of objects. We have preserved the original apparent denotation by changing the connotation of the word 'real'.

So now we can relax our earlier severity, and admit that there *is* a sense in which the qualities a thing has are those presented to a normal observer under standard conditions. We might even call these the *sensible* qualities of things as opposed to the *true* qualities of the thing, whatever science finally decides the true qualities are. But, of course, we must insist that this new sense of 'real' is a quite subsidiary and parasitic sense of the word, a sense which is quite compatible with saying that the object does not *really* have these properties at all. For we are only admitting that it is linguistically convenient to call certain widespread illusions 'genuine perceptions' for the purposes of ordinary life. From the point of view of metaphysics the ordinary usage is misleading, and could be replaced by a distinction between different sorts of perceptual illusion.

After the offer of this Greek gift to Phenomenalism, we may also be encouraged to take a more relaxed attitude to such 'entities' as mirror-images. We argued before that there are no such *things* as mirror-images, although the word 'mirror-image' has a use in describing certain very common and semi-public sensory illusions. For when we look into a mirror there is no such object behind the surface of the glass as our eyes would incline us to believe; while if mirror-images are taken to be perceptions of an object in *front* of the glass (e.g. ourselves), it has to be admitted that the object is perceived subject to certain distortions. But our new tolerance of speech towards systematic illusion, where it seems to exist in the case of the drop of blood or the surface of the table, may also give us a more tolerant attitude to mirror-images. We may now be prepared to say that there is *a* sense in which they are real, because all normal perceivers 'perceive' mirror-images under certain definite conditions. The only difference from the case of the blood and the table is that we can find reason for treating mirror-images as illusions *without doing any physics*. Common sense tells us that there can be no object like the one there seems to be behind the glass of the mirror, but it needs a great deal of physical research to discover that the table is not really continuous. But we can, if we want to, easily ignore this difference, and treat *both* as 'realities' in the ordinary world of perception.

It will be seen that we have made no real concession of doctrine here. We have simply made linguistic concessions which may be found soothing, and which may show that Phenomenalism does have *some* rationale, however much its adherents misunderstand that rationale. In the important sense of the word 'illusory', we are still maintaining that we can, if evidence offers, reject as illusory the so-called paradigm cases of veridical perception. But we admit now that there is a *subsidiary* sense of the word 'illusory' in which this is not so, viz. where 'illusory' means 'not what is perceived by normal observers in standard conditions'.

14

PROBLEMS ABOUT THE
SECONDARY QUALITIES

THE world view we are now considering, and endeavouring to reconcile with Direct Realism, extrudes the 'secondary' qualities of colour, sound, taste, smell, and perhaps heat and cold, from the physical world, on the ground that no natural place for them can be found in physical theory. This raises serious difficulties which must now be considered.

I. THE APPARENT SIMPLICITY OF THE SECONDARY QUALITIES

We have seen that if we give a Realistic account of the physicist's 'fundamental particles' we shall have to say that physical objects which *look to have* or *feel to have* a continuous surface do not really have such a surface. In the case of a table the 'fundamental particles' may be more closely packed together than in the case of objects that do not even *look* to have a continuous surface. But they remain separated. Nevertheless, at least we could give an account of what a continuous surface would be like, if it did exist, *in terms of objects that have a real existence*. For if it were possible to pack 'fundamental particles' together so that there was no empty space between them, then we would have a surface that really was continuous.

But the difficulty about such qualities as colour, if a Realistic interpretation of atomic physics is correct, is that we can give *no* account of what we mean by saying that a surface is coloured red in terms of objects that have a real existence. Of course, if we accept a Representative theory of perception, the problem is easily solved. We can say that colours are qualities qualifying our sense-impressions, although wrongly taken by unreflective and un-scientific common sense to qualify physical surfaces. But we have offered an account of what it is to have a sense-impression, arguing that it is no more than having a belief or inclination to believe that we are perceiving something physical. To have a red sense-impression, on this view, is to have a belief or inclination to believe that we are perceiving a physical object with a red surface. Now what do we mean by a *red* surface? If we take the physicist's theories in a Realistic way, then it seems there are no red things in the world. What is worse, it does not seem possible to give an account of what a red thing would be like in terms of things that do exist. There is a sharp asymmetry here between the notion of an absolutely continuous surface, of which we could give an account in terms of the packing together of 'fundamental par-ticles', and the notion of a red surface. But if the quality of redness is never instantiated, and if we can give no account of what red-ness is in terms of properties that are instantiated, can we give the word 'red' any meaning? Certainly it would seem impossible for two people to know that 'red' had the same meaning for them both, or even for one person to know that the word had the same meaning for him on two different occasions. For how could there even be a possibility of deciding, in the case of doubt, that the word was being used in the same way? But if there are no ways of deciding the word has the same meaning, how can we give a sense to saying the word has any meaning at all?

The trouble is, of course, that the secondary qualities seem to be, in some sense, *simple* qualities, with the consequence that we are unable to give an account of them in terms of anything else.[1] They seem to be 'intractable', there seems to be no prospect of re-ducing them to anything else, or exhibiting them as constructions

[1] In *Philosophical Investigations*, secs. 46–48 Wittgenstein seems to be denying that the distinction between simple and complex can ever be anything but a distinction relative to some standard by which simplicity and complexity are judged. Nevertheless, the secondary qualities do *appear* to be simple in some absolute sense, presenting 'one simple uniform appearance or conception in the mind', as Locke puts it (*Essay*, II, 2, 1.). At the very least, this impres-sion that the secondary qualities make on us must be explained before we can accept Wittgenstein's view. It is this apparent simplicity of the secondary qualities which helps to give Logical Atomism its attractions.

out of simpler elements. Compare the property of 'being a horse' with the property of 'being yellow'. We normally learn the word 'horse' by ostensive teaching, and it would certainly be no easy matter to give a definition of a horse. But the task does not seem inherently impossible, as it does in the case of yellow. Perhaps no definition we could find would ever map our usage of the word 'horse' with any exactitude. But some sort of a definition could be found which would be some use in explaining what a horse was to somebody who did not know. But, in the case of yellow, it seems that we could find nothing at all that would even begin to do the job. The reason is clear. We think of a horse as being essentially a complex structure involving many different parts and qualities in all sorts of complex relations to each other. There seems no such complexity to be found in the case of yellow.

2. ARE THE SECONDARY QUALITIES REALLY SIMPLE?

Nevertheless, before we conclude that we have found a serious objection to the combination of a Direct Realist theory of perception with a Realistic account of atomic physics, we ought to notice that there are reasons for saying that the secondary qualities are not simple, but have, as it were, a *hidden* complexity in them.

These reasons are nothing more than the notorious fact that the secondary qualities stand in quite complex logical relations to each other. It follows from the nature of the qualities in question that blue resembles purple more than it resembles red. Furthermore it follows from the nature of colour that two different colours cannot qualify the same surface or volume at the same time (although the very same object can be red and round, or red and sweet, it cannot be red and green). Logical relations between other ranges of the secondary qualities are not so clear-cut and obvious, but they seem to exist also.[1] Now how could these relations between different qualities exist, relations apparently based solely on the intrinsic nature of the qualities related, unless there were some

[1] It is a very interesting and curious fact that these logical relations between various secondary qualities seem to hold only between qualities discerned *by the same sense*. It is true that we do make certain connections 'across the senses'. Locke's blind man who likened scarlet to the sound of a trumpet strikes us as having made a shrewd remark. But these connections seem to be mere *associative* links (perhaps based on emotional reactions), not flowing from the intrinsic nature of the two qualities connected.

inner complexity in the qualities themselves to support these different relations? If these qualities really were simple, it seems that we could say no more about them except that they were all different from each other. The existence of relations that hold between some qualities and not between others, relations based solely on the nature of the related terms, bears witness to their complexity.

At this stage, we should take brief notice of a contrary opinion. In a footnote to his chapter on Abstract Ideas in the *Treatise* Hume writes:

> It is evident, that even different simple ideas may have a similarity or resemblance to each other; nor is it necessary, that the point or circumstance of resemblance should be distinct or separable from that in which they differ. *Blue* or *green* are different simple ideas, but are more resembling than *blue* or *scarlet*; though their perfect simplicity excludes all possibility of separation or distinction. It is the same case with particular sounds, and tastes and smells. These admit of infinite resemblances upon the general appearance and comparison, without any circumstance the same.[1]

The whole question is very difficult, but I am inclined to reject Hume's view. Consider the three colours, yellow, orange and red. Yellow has a certain resemblance to orange, a resemblance involved in the nature of yellow and orange, but it lacks that resemblance to red. Red has a certain resemblance to orange, a resemblance involved in the nature of red and orange, but it lacks that resemblance to yellow. This implies that orange is such that it supports two different relations of resemblance. But, since these relations of resemblance are determined by the intrinsic nature of orange, this intrinsic nature seems to involve complexity. And following out this line of argument by considering other examples, we might be led to think that there were none of the secondary qualities that did not involve complexity, even though superficial reflection may pronounce them simple.

We may be strengthened in this opinion if we remember that the other view of the matter was inevitable for Hume, who takes the secondary qualities to qualify our sense-impressions, and takes sense-impressions to be as they appear to be. Since these qualities *appear* to be simple, they must *be* simple. Yet, at the same time, if

[1] Vol. I, bk. I, sec. VII, p. 28 Everyman edition.

the simple quality blue seems to resemble green more than scarlet, that must be true too.

3. CAN THE SECONDARY QUALITIES BE REDUCED TO PRIMARY QUALITIES?

But even if Hume is wrong, and if the secondary qualities do have a concealed complexity in their nature so that we can give some sort of definition or analysis of them, it may seem that this does nothing to solve our present difficulties. A definition or account of, say, redness, would presumably have to be given in terms of other properties which are also excluded from the physicist's account of physical reality. The same problem that we raised about redness would then arise about these other properties. No account could be given of them in terms of what the physicist takes to be the real properties of physical objects, nor would it be compatible with our Direct Realism to make them properties of sense-impressions. For to have a sense-impression, we have argued, is simply to think we are perceiving something in the physical world.

At this stage, however, we must remember the persistent attempts that have been made throughout the history of thought to give an account of the secondary qualities in terms of the primary qualities. Perhaps we had better re-examine these attempts.

The traditional attempts to give an account of the secondary qualities in terms of primary qualities, made by many scientists and a few philosophers, have depended on identifying the secondary qualities with different sorts of *motions*. Thus, colours have been identified with light-waves or with movements in the optic nerve or cortex, sounds with sound-waves or movements in the auditory nerves or cortex, and so on. The traditional objection to these identifications is that to associate the colour red with a certain wave-length is to put forward a synthetic proposition, because we could quite well imagine the one existing without the other. A man blind from birth could understand what a wavelength was quite easily, but could hardly make a beginning at understanding what redness was. This objection seems to me to be conclusive.

Recently, however, a much more sophisticated account of the secondary qualities in terms of the primary qualities of objects has been proposed by J. J. C. Smart, an account which is by no means so obviously unsatisfactory, however serious the objections to it may be. Smart's position is briefly sketched in an article 'Sensations and Brain Processes'.[1] I quote from the article:

> I must therefore digress for a moment and indicate how I deal with secondary qualities. I shall concentrate on colour.
>
> First of all, let me introduce the concept of a normal percipient. One person is more a normal percipient than another if he can make colour discriminations that the other cannot. For example, if A can pick a lettuce leaf out of a heap of cabbage leaves, whereas B cannot though he can pick a lettuce leaf out of a heap of beetroot leaves, then A is more normal than B. (I am assuming that A and B are not given time to distinguish the leaves by their slight differences in shape, and so forth.) From the concept of 'more normal than' it is easy to see how we can introduce the concept of 'normal'. Of course, Eskimos may make the finest discriminations at the blue end of the spectrum, Hottentots at the red end. In this case the concept of a normal percipient is a slightly idealized one, rather like that of 'the mean sun' in astronomical chronology. There is no need to go into such subtleties now. I say that 'This is red' means something roughly like 'A normal percipient would not easily pick this out of a clump of geranium petals though he would pick it out of a clump of lettuce leaves'. Of course it does not exactly mean this: a person might know the meaning of 'red' without knowing anything about geraniums, or normal percipients. But the point is that a person can be trained to say 'This is red' of objects which would not be easily picked out of geranium petals by a normal percipient, and so on. (Note that even a colour-blind person can reasonably assert that something is red, though of course he needs to use another human being, not just himself, as his 'colour-meter'.) This account of secondary qualities explains their unimportance in physics. For obviously the discriminations and lack of discriminations made by a very complex neurophysiological mechanism are hardly likely to correspond to simple and non-arbitrary distinctions in nature.
>
> I therefore elucidate colours as powers, in Locke's sense, to evoke certain sorts of discriminatory responses in human beings.

An account can then be given of the nervous systems of the human beings that do the discriminating, and the objects dis-

[1] *Philosophical Review*, vol. LXVIII, 1959, pp. 149–150. I have also had the advantage of reading unpublished material by Professor Smart on this topic, and of discussing some of the issues with him.

criminated, purely in terms of the primary qualities. Where discriminating responses are not normal, then we have what is ordinarily called misperception of the secondary qualities of objects.

Suppose there are a number of pieces of cloth which are not discriminable in respect of shade, size or texture, but that some of them are a certain shade of blue, while others are a certain shade of green. I am a normal percipient and I succeed in sorting the pieces of cloth according to their colour. According to Smart it would be misleading to say that I make a distinction between the two classes on the basis of their different colour. Rather, my making a separation between the two classes is one of the things that makes me say that they are of a different colour. The separation logically precedes the colour-difference, not the colour-difference the separation. To be a piece of cloth of a different colour from another *means* that I do such things as putting the pieces of cloth in different piles.

But now, it will be objected, there must be a real difference between the pieces of blue and green cloth, otherwise we would not *make a difference* between them, use words like 'same' and 'different' in a certain way, and, in general, react to the pieces of cloth differently. Smart, I take it, would reply to this by saying that there are real differences in the two sorts of cloth, differences in their primary qualities, although probably no simple or clearcut differences. These differences affect the very complicated mechanism that is our brain and nervous system in different ways, causing our differences in reaction. But the criteria for 'blueness' and 'greenness' are *the way we react to the objects*, in particular the discriminations we are able to make, and not *that in the objects that causes this difference of reaction*.

Smart can then explain the apparent simplicity of the secondary qualities in terms of the simplicity of our discriminatory responses when, for instance, we distinguish between the two sorts of cloth which are identical in all but colour. If some of the pieces of cloth of each colour were warm and some cold we would have two possible methods of discrimination, into blues and greens or into hots and colds. But in the original case there is only one possible method of discrimination using the secondary qualities, viz. difference of colour. Smart can now say that talk about the simplicity of blue and green simply amounts to our preparedness to sort the pieces of cloth in only one way, our ability to make only one sort of discrimination.

Colour-incompatibilities can then be explained in terms of *different* simple discriminatory responses. To treat a thing as both red and green all over would be to respond to it by two incompatible responses. Thus, if a green thing can be picked out from geraniums but not from lettuces, while a red thing can be picked out from lettuces but not from geraniums, a thing that was both red and green would be something that could and could not be picked out from lettuces and geraniums, which is nonsense.

Finally, statements like 'Orange is more like red, than yellow is like red' can be translated by saying that it is harder to discriminate between an orange and a red thing, than between a yellow and a red thing. The criterion of the resemblance or difference of 'simple' secondary qualities is thus reduced to our relative inability or ability to discriminate between certain things. Smart thus seems to be able to explain the 'simplicity' of the secondary qualities, their 'resemblances', and their 'incompatibilities', which certainly represents a quite striking achievement for his theory of the secondary qualities. (It may be that difficulties would appear for the theory if we tried to work out these points in a more detailed way, just as in the case of Phenomenalism. But the theory wears a reasonably promising aspect.)

At this point it may be objected that it is perfectly possible, perfectly imaginable, that without any change in their primary qualities, all the objects that are blue should be green, and vice versa. Here we would still react differently to the two sorts of objects, would still discriminate between them as before, and yet we would be dealing with a different situation. This seems incompatible with an account of the colours as nothing but powers to evoke certain sorts of discriminatory response in us.

I suppose that Smart would reply to this by saying that here we err by treating 'blue' and 'green' in isolation from the other colours. If grass became blue and forget-me-nots green, there would still be an observable difference in the situation, even on his theory. For grass would be harder to distinguish from purple objects than it was before, and forget-me-nots easier. So it is not clear that this is a conclusive objection.

If we accepted Smart's account of the secondary qualities, we should have to reject our own analysis of sensory illusion in the case of secondary qualities. For, on his view, to 'misperceive' secondary qualities is simply to exhibit abnormal responses.

A secondary quality of an object is something like the foulness of a toadstool. We react with disgust to the 'foul' toadstool, we react with certain discriminatory responses to the 'coloured' object. But the reactions constitute the foulness and the colour. Some people do not react to toadstools with disgust, others react to 'coloured' objects with unusual discriminatory responses. We *say* that such people misperceive colours, but we only mean that their reactions are abnormal.

But we could continue to accept our own account of sensory illusion with respect to the *primary* qualities. And so we could continue our attempt to reconcile a Direct Realist theory of perception with a Realistic account of atomic physics by saying, for example, that everybody is under sensory illusion when the surfaces of tables look to them to be continuous. We would simply be freed from the necessity of saying anything like this in the case of the secondary qualities. We would not have to say that everybody is under the illusion that objects are coloured, have tastes and smells, etc. For, since people make the discriminatory responses to objects that they do make, it follows on Smart's theory that objects are coloured, have tastes, smells, etc. Yet this would stand in no contradiction to the physicist's account of reality.

Nevertheless, there remain some very serious difficulties for Smart's account of the secondary qualities.

(i) Suppose, as seems possible, that there was a range of secondary qualities, never before perceived, and that the members of this range 'mapped' the colours, standing to each other in just the formal relations that the colours stand to each other (there will be exact formal analogies to 'Purple is between blue and red', 'Nothing can be red and green all over', etc.). Suppose now that these qualities came to qualify the objects that colours had previously qualified, the primary qualities of the objects remaining the same, so that each colour was replaced by the corresponding member of the new range. Suppose also that we perceived these qualities by means of the eyes, as we now perceive colours. Objects having these qualities would evoke exactly the same discriminatory responses in us as colours did before, yet, by hypothesis, they would not be colours.

I think Smart would meet this difficulty by distinguishing

between discriminatory responses towards objects and *sensations*. When we perceive the colours of objects, we not only make certain discriminatory responses, but we also have certain colour-sensations. These colour-sensations he goes on to identify with *brain-processes*. Our imagined case of a new range of qualities replacing the colours would be a case where our discriminatory responses stayed the same, but our sensations were no longer *colour*-sensations. In other words, the brain processes accompanying our discriminatory responses would be different. If this exceedingly hard doctrine were accepted, Smart might be able to meet our present objection.

Smart's only alternative would be to deny that there could be a second range of qualities 'mapping' the colours; to assert that the 'second' range would be the colours all over again. But this reply seems equally implausible.

(ii) A second serious difficulty for Smart's account of the secondary qualities is the wide gap that it puts between them and the primary qualities. According to Smart, an object's length, say, is an intrinsic property of the object. But its colour is a mere power in the object to cause us to make certain discriminations, to say 'the same' or 'different' in certain contexts, to pick out the object in certain contexts and to fail to pick it out in other contexts. This asymmetry in the accounts given of the two sets of qualities seems quite extraordinary. We should be naturally inclined to say they are *both* intrinsic qualities of the object. Here we may revive the criticism that Berkeley made of Locke, viz. that whatever account is given of the secondary qualities must hold of the primary qualities too. (Berkeley draws the moral that since Locke admits the secondary qualities to be mere subjective sense-impressions he ought to admit the same of the primary qualities.) Following Berkeley, we could argue that, if the secondary qualities are mere powers in objects to cause us to make certain discriminations, then we should extend the same doctrine to the primary qualities, a conclusion which would leave the intrinsic nature of objects quite unknowable.

It seems insufficient for Smart to reply that physicists have discovered that they can get a coherent theory of reality if they treat the primary qualities as real qualities of objects, but cannot do so in the case of the secondary qualities. In their own nature we find no marks of inferiority to the primary qualities, no reason why we should analyse them as mere powers to cause reactions in us. If Smart's view were correct, a philosopher should be able to demonstrate this feature of the logic of secondary qualities even without knowing anything about the facts science discovers.

Now it might be replied here that a logical distinction between the primary and the secondary qualities can easily be discovered. We find out what a thing's real length is by an objective technique, viz. measurement. But we find out a thing's 'real' colour by appealing to the verdict of the many. If, under standard conditions, a thing looks to be blue to the great majority of perceivers, that settles the matter: the thing is blue. Now difference in the method of verification of claims about the two sorts of qualities implies a difference in their nature. Measurement implies objectivity, reliance on the mob, subjectivity.

However, although it is certainly true that we settle disputes about colours in this rough-and-ready way in ordinary practice, this seems to be a contingent fact. It would be perfectly possible to decide such disputes by reference to a carefully constructed colour-chart put alongside the surface whose colour is to be determined, just as a ruler is placed alongside the object whose length is to be determined. It is no objection to this method of determining colour that we would have to *see* that the coloured surface had the same colour as the sample on the chart, thus bringing in the possibility of illusion. For in the case of the ruler, it is necessary to *see* that the thing to be measured coincides with points on the ruler, so that there is a possibility of illusion here too. But if this reliance on perception does nothing to cast doubt on the objectivity of lengths, it should do nothing to cast doubt on the objectivity of colours either.

So it seems that no real differences have emerged in the way we speak about primary and secondary qualities. Hence Smart cannot justify the startlingly different account of the two groups of qualities that he wishes to give. It is not enough for him to say that physicists find the secondary qualities difficult to fit into their world-picture, for this is not a conceptual point, it has no bearing on the logical status of these qualities. Of course, the physicists' difficulties might make us suspect that there is some conceptual point to be discovered about the secondary qualities. But, so far, no relevant point of difference from the primary qualities has been discovered.

(iii) The third objection is a reason for rejecting *any* account of physical objects which allows them only the primary qualities. I propose to leave it until the next chapter.

I think we must therefore reject Smart's account of the secondary qualities. I do so with some regret, because, if it were correct, certain very difficult problems connected with the secondary qualities (e.g. the problem of colour-incompatibilities) would find a simple and straightforward solution. But I do not see how to overcome the two difficulties already proposed, and the further problem to be brought up in the next chapter.

If this is so, our attempt to reconcile a Direct Realist theory of perception with a Realistic account of atomic physics has come to grief over the problem of the secondary qualities. If we cannot give an account of these secondary qualities in terms of the primary ones; and, if we reject the view that they qualify 'mental objects' such as sense-impressions; we are left with the conclusion that objects appear to be coloured, have tastes and smells, emit sounds, etc., yet never in fact possess any of these qualities. But, as we saw at the beginning of this chapter, in that case we cannot understand what it is to attribute these qualities to objects. For since they appear to be *simple* qualities, or, if complex, to be complexes of simpler secondary qualities, we cannot give an account of the meaning of words like 'red', 'blue', 'sour', in terms of anything that exists at all.

It seems, then, that we must find some place for the secondary qualities as qualities of physical objects. This means that we cannot accept the physicist's view of physical reality as it stands.

15

CAN PHYSICAL OBJECTS HAVE NOTHING BUT THE PRIMARY QUALITIES?

I SHALL now propose an argument to show that it is logically impossible for a physical object to have nothing but the primary qualities. The argument is present in embryo in Berkeley's *Principles*,[1] but it is more clearly stated by Hume.[2]

It will be convenient to begin by considering the list of primary qualities proposed by Descartes, and the one addition to this list proposed by Locke. The qualities recognised by modern physics include all the Cartesian qualities, together with some others. It will be shown, however, that these additions do not enable us to evade the difficulties that face Descartes and Locke.

Descartes says that the primary or real properties of matter are shape, size, position, duration, movability, divisibility and number.[3] This list we can immediately diminish by one, because it is clear that *number* is an interloper here. A physical object has not got a number in the way it has a shape, size, position, duration and velocity. It makes sense to say that an object is round or at rest, but it makes no sense to say that it is three. Only if we say that it is three pounds in weight, or made of three pieces of wood, do we have an intelligible assertion. Only when we have *specified a unit* does our attribution of number become meaningful. So to

---

[1] *Principles of Human Knowledge*, sec. 10.
[2] *Treatise*, bk. I, part IV, sec. 4 'Of the Modern Philosophy'.
[3] Cf. the second paragraph in the Fifth Meditation, and elsewhere.

speak of physical objects as having number is not really to characterise their nature at all.

But what of the remainder of the list? Do these qualities suffice
to give us a physical object? It seems to me they do not, and I
shall try to bring this out by showing that these qualities just by
themselves do not suffice to differentiate a physical object from
empty space.[1] Descartes' view would make a thing indistinguishable from a vacuum. If this can be made good, it seems a sufficient
criticism.

In the first place, we can speak of the shape, size and duration of
an empty space or vacuum just as much as that of a physical object,
so there is no differentiating mark there. Somebody who accepted
the Relational theory of space might point out here that the notion
of a vacuum, on this theory, is logically subsequent to the objects
that environ it. This is true, but not to the point. Granting this, we
do, or could, speak of the shape, size and duration of both
physical objects and vacua. (For instance, we could teach a child
what length was by comparing different distances between
physical things, even though those distances were vacuous.) So if
physical objects are more than vacua they must have some *further*
property to differentiate them.

Position will not suffice for this further property. If we accept
a doctrine of Absolute space, then it is clear that an unoccupied
portion of that space will have absolute position just as much as
one occupied by a physical object. If, alternatively, we take the
Relational view that a thing's spatial position is constituted by its
spatial relations *to other physical objects*, then it is clear also that
position cannot serve as a differentiating property of physical
objects. For in order to understand the notion of position we
would already have to understand the notion of a physical object.
(The same points apply to position in *time* also.)

It might seem that motion would be a sufficient differentiating
mark to distinguish between physical objects and mere empty
space. For although a physical object is capable of motion, it is not
clear what, if anything, the motion of an empty space would come
to. But what is motion? A body is in motion if it is in a series of
adjoining places at successive times. That is all that motion is.

---

[1] It may be objected that no differentiating *qualities* are necessary, but only
the presence of a physical object. This objection will be considered shortly,
after we have developed our argument further.

(Similarly, rest is simply being at the same place at successive times.) Now this means that we can give an analysis of motion solely in terms of the concepts of shape, size, position and duration. It is not a new primitive concept. But we have already examined these concepts, and have found that, even when they are taken together, they are insufficient to differentiate physical objects from empty space. We will still want to know what is the nature of that which is in a series of adjoining places during successive times.

Finally, divisibility fails to constitute a differentiating mark. To say a thing is divisible is to say that it is capable of being broken up or separated into two or more *things*. Clearly, this will not serve to define, or help to define, the nature of a thing, any more than it will help to define a cat to say it is the offspring of two cats.

We may conclude, therefore, that it is logically impossible that a physical object should have none but the Cartesian primary qualities. Descartes himself seems to have been half-aware of the difficulties his theory faced, and tried to overcome them by boldly identifying matter and space, and, as a consequence, denying the possibility of a vacuum. He relied on *motion* to break up the plenum and give us distinct physical objects. But we have already seen that motion by itself could not accomplish this task, for motion is analysable in terms of purely spatial and temporal concepts.

Perhaps Locke had some awareness of Descartes' difficulties on this point, and this may have induced him to fill out the Cartesian list of primary qualities by adding *solidity*.[1] By 'solidity' Locke says that he means:

> That which . . . hinders the approach of two bodies, when they are moved one towards another, . . .

He considers the suggestion that 'impenetrability' would be a better term, but says:

> Only I have thought the term solidity the more proper to express this idea, not only because of its vulgar use in that sense, but also because it carries more of something positive in it than impenetrability; which is negative, and is perhaps more a consequence of solidity, than solidity itself.

[1] *Essay*, bk. II, chap. 4, 'Idea of Solidity'.

But in fact it seems that this is a distinction without a difference, because Locke means by solidity 'that which is impenetrable'. The ideas of solidity and impenetrability are tautologically connected.

But if solidity is simply impenetrability it is clear that Locke has failed to patch up Descartes' theory. For, although it is not very clear just what Locke means by impenetrability (he explicitly distinguishes it from *hardness*), it is clear that impenetrability is a relation, and a relation that one physical object has to another physical object.[1] But if this is so, we cannot make it a differentiating mark of a physical object, or part of a differentiating mark, on pain of circularity. So Locke's attempt to bolster up the Cartesian position is unsuccessful. (His attempt to escape from 'impenetrability' into 'solidity' may involve some vague realisation of this.)

The moral to be drawn from this failure of Descartes and Locke to present a coherent doctrine of the nature of physical objects is that objects must have at least one further quality over and above the qualities on the Cartesian or Lockean lists. It is not necessary that this quality be one of those which they dismiss as secondary, for it might be some unknown quality. But there must be at least one extra quality. Furthermore this extra quality, or these extra qualities, must pass two tests.

The first test is this. The new quality, or qualities, must not be analysable solely in terms of the Cartesian–Lockean list. We have already applied this criticism to the concept of motion, and another example, I think, would be the qualities of softness and hardness. When Locke distinguishes impenetrability and hardness he says that the latter is:

> a firm cohesion of the parts of matter, making up masses of a sensible bulk, so that the whole does not easily change its figure.

Now, accepting Locke's account of hardness, this means that it is a disposition of a thing not to change its figure easily. (While softness is the opposite disposition.) But if this is correct, then we have given an analysis of hardness solely in terms of two qualities in the original Cartesian list, shape and size. Hardness (and softness) could not therefore be candidates for the additional qualities that are needed to eke out Descartes' and Locke's list.

The second test to be passed is that the new quality or qualities must not be relations that physical objects have to other physical

[1] Cf. Hume, op. cit.

objects. (We might indeed argue that they must not be *any* sort of relation, but the weaker thesis will suffice here.)[1] Once again, we have already applied this criticism to various concepts: position, divisibility, and impenetrability. The property of *weight* is another example. It is clear that the weight of a physical object is *constituted* by its relations to other objects, or its capacity to enter into certain relations with other objects. For instance, the heavier a thing is, that is, the more it weighs, the further it will depress a spring-balance. Doubtless there is no one *particular* relation or capacity for a relation between objects which constitutes their weight. But weight seems to be no more than the whole complex of operations by which we find out a thing's weight, and these operations are all a matter of discovering that certain relations hold between the object to be weighed and other objects. This is shown by the fact that we cannot understand the supposition that a thing should change its weight, while its relations to everything else, including its relations to balances, remain the same. So we could not add weight alone to the Cartesian and Lockean list and have a coherent conception of a physical object.

Now if we turn to modern physics, we shall find that the 'fundamental particles' of modern theory are credited with a few more properties than those found in the Cartesian or Lockean list or derivable from this list. In particular, they are said to have mass and electric charge. But mass and electric charge, when scrutinised, seem also to dissolve into relations, or dispositions to have relations, that one particle has to another particle. The result is that the modern theory, if it is taken as a literal account of physical reality, is in no better position than the Cartesian or Lockean theory. Physical objects must have at least one further quality, a quality that can negotiate our two tests.

Well, what known qualities could pass the tests? Examination reveals a surprisingly short list of plausible candidates. Colours, sounds, tastes, smells, heat and cold, it is plausible to say, cannot be analysed in terms of the Cartesian–Lockean list, nor do they seem to involve relations that one thing has to another thing. (Of course, if Smart's account of the secondary qualities were correct, even these qualities would fail to pass the tests.) But I cannot find any other qualities of physical objects that fulfil these conditions.

[1] Our argument will shortly require an appeal to the stronger thesis, when we consider an objection to our whole line of argument here.

So it seems that we must either fill out the physicist's account of physical objects by treating colours, etc., as real properties of objects (to pick and choose among them seems arbitrary); or else we must postulate further qualities 'I know not what' which, as it were, provide the stuffing for physical objects.

It might be objected here that no qualities are necessary. What occupies space is a material object or substance. If we ask what is the difference between a physical object and empty space we can only say that a physical object *fills* space, that no two material objects can be in exactly the same place, that is to say, that a physical object is impenetrable. But there is nothing more to be said. The physical object is material, it is substantial, it is a thing, it is a physical object. If we do not understand the difference between a material object and empty space there is nothing else that could make us understand it. In particular, to talk about *qualities* is quite unnecessary. Reference to qualities could not explain the difference between a physical object and empty space.

But we could hardly accept the conception of a physical object without *any* properties, a substance without accidents. If we say that a physical object differs from empty space by possessing the property of impenetrability, then we must remember that impenetrability is some sort of *relational* property. The question then arises what nature, what qualities, the physical object has in itself, apart from its relations to other things. The nature of physical things cannot be exhausted by their relations to other material things, they must have some *intrinsic*, non-relational, qualities. Shape, size, and duration are perhaps intrinsic properties; but they, as we have seen, fail to differentiate physical objects from empty spaces. The only possible candidates for intrinsic qualities seem to be (*a*) the known secondary qualities, (*b*) further unknown qualities.[1]

If we say that physical objects possess unknown (although not unknowable) qualities, as J. J. C. Smart has tentatively proposed, we shall be faced with two problems. In the first place we shall

---

[1] If it is objected that the secondary qualities do nothing to give physical objects one of their essential characteristics viz. impenetrability, the reply is that, even if this is true, it is irrelevant. Our argument is designed to show only that physical objects must have secondary qualities or further unknown qualities, if a distinction is to be made between physical objects and empty space. We have not argued that such qualities are sufficient for a physical object.

have to give some satisfactory account of the secondary qualities. In the second place, we shall have to accept the paradox that we know absolutely nothing of the intrinsic nature of physical objects, except their spatial properties. Our knowledge would be limited solely to the relations that one object has to another. However, we would be able to accept the world-picture of modern physics as a literal account of the nature of reality, subject only to scientific correction.

But since we have rejected a reductive analysis of the secondary qualities I am inclined to say that some place for these 'secondary' qualities will have to be found in the physicist's account of physical reality. One important point here is that it need not be assumed that physical objects have just those secondary qualities they seem to have. In the previous chapters, we saw no logical objection to saying that sensory illusion is a much more widespread affair than common sense assumes or admits in its speech. And if the physicist's account of reality is literally true it is certain that our ordinary perceptions of the *primary* qualities regularly involve a great deal of illusion. So might not this be true of the secondary qualities *also*? Might not physics be able to produce a theory which correlated real secondary qualities of the true 'fundamental particles' with their real primary qualities *in a simple way*? And if so, what objection would there be to admitting these qualities into an account of physical reality?

But all this, I must admit, is very tentative. In our discussion whether it is possible to reconcile a Direct Realist account of perception with a Realistic account of modern physics we have found difficulties that we have not been able to solve. Further investigation of the problem of the 'secondary qualities' is called for. Perhaps what is really required is a more satisfying account of the nature of a physical object. Perhaps, behind the problems of knowledge we have been investigating, lies the deeper problem of substance.

CONCLUSION

NOW that we have reached the end of our argument, let us sum up our positive results.

Physical objects or happenings stimulate our sense-organs. As a causal result of this, we acquire immediate knowledge of their existence and their properties. By *immediate* knowledge is meant knowledge which is not inferred from, or suggested by, any further knowledge, or any ground or basis for knowledge. This knowledge is not necessarily verbalised knowledge, but it is always knowledge which it is logically possible to put verbally. It is propositional in form. And although such knowledge is immediate, in the sense just defined, it is not incorrigible knowledge.

As a result of the stimulation of the eye, we acquire immediate knowledge of the size, shape, colour and spatial relations of the objects in our environment; as a result of the stimulation of the skin, we acquire immediate knowledge of the shape, size, temperature, spatial relations, and other properties of the objects in our environment; as a result of the stimulation of the nose, we acquire immediate knowledge of the presence of smells; and so on. After we gain some knowledge of the world, this knowledge is accompanied by knowledge of the means by which this immediate knowledge was got (by the eyes, skin, nose, etc.). It is also regularly accompanied by characteristic *sensations* in the organs being used to acquire the immediate knowledge.

The acquiring of immediate knowledge in this fashion is *perception*. It may be distinguished from more sophisticated forms of perception by being called *immediate* perception. But it must be emphasized that immediate perception is not immediate knowledge. It is the *acquiring* of immediate knowledge, and is therefore an *event* in the sense that an acquiring is an event.

It is part of our concept of immediate perception that the knowledge acquired is knowledge of the state of affairs in the physical world *contemporary* with the acquiring of the knowledge. This logical necessity is built on the empirical fact that we never acquire any *immediate* knowledge of past states of affairs by means of the senses.

The objects and properties of objects that are immediately perceived have an existence logically independent of their being perceived. They may be perceived or not perceived. There are objects and properties of objects that are never perceived, although it would always be logically possible for such unperceived things to be perceived. Our theory is therefore Realistic.

This acquiring of immediate knowledge by means of the senses regularly gives rise, by a process of suggestion (automatic transition from one belief to an associated belief), to the acquiring of further beliefs about the world. For instance, if I have sufficient experience, the immediate acquiring of the knowledge that there is at present a black thing of a certain shape in my environment brings with it the further knowledge that there is a cat before me. This mediate acquiring of knowledge may be called *mediate* perception. In developed perception, there is no absolutely sharp distinction between immediate and mediate acquirings of knowledge.

These acquirings of immediate and mediate knowledge are usually *conscious*. That is to say, we are usually aware of acquiring the knowledge at the time, although our perceptions are not always the centre of our attention. We can, however, perceive unconsciously, as in the case where somebody shows that he has acquired the knowledge of what was written on a hoarding, although he did not realise that he saw the lettering on the hoarding when his eyes were resting on it.

On some occasions, our sense-organs or nervous system may be stimulated in such a way that we immediately acquire false beliefs about the world of the same general sort as the true beliefs acquired in immediate perception. This is immediate sensory illusion. It may give rise to mediate sensory illusion.

In some cases of immediate sensory illusion, however, we do not acquire false beliefs, but only *inclinations to false beliefs*. (The same thing can happen, though it is rare, in the case of veridical perception. We acquire a mere inclination to a true belief.) The inclination to believe is a thought about the world that would necessarily be a belief, but for the fact that it is inhibited by previously acquired knowledge which holds the thought in check.

(Such acquiring of immediate inclination to a false belief *may* lead to the mediate perception of the real state of affairs. An example is to be found in the use of mirrors.)

If we restrict ourselves to our *conscious* and *immediate* perceptions, that is, our conscious and immediate acquirings of beliefs or inclinations to believe propositions about the physical world, acquired as a result of stimulation of our senses or nervous system; and if we abstract both from the truth or falsity of these perceptions and from whether they are beliefs or mere inclinations to believe; we have what are called our *sense-impressions*. But these sense-impressions are not evidence or basis for our immediate knowledge of the physical world, they are simply our immediate impressions of the world. (The properties attributed to sense-impressions—such as indeterminacy—are really characteristics of the beliefs or inclinations to believe that are acquired when we 'have certain sense-impressions'.) Since sense-impressions do not stand between us and our immediate knowledge of the world, our theory is a *Direct* Realism.

If we accept this account of perception, yet also wish to accept a Realistic account of modern physics, we must say that what common sense accounts to be veridical perceptions involve unsuspected illusory elements, that is, involve the acquiring of unsuspected false beliefs. (In ordinary life, however, it may be convenient to go on calling such perceptions 'veridical', because we want to mark them off from what are *ordinarily* treated as non-veridical perceptions. But then the meaning of the word 'veridical' has changed.)

If we further accept a reductive account of the 'secondary qualities', in terms of the abilities of perceivers to make certain discriminations between physical things, we shall have to revise our account of perception with respect to the secondary qualities. For, on this account, to perceive secondary qualities is simply to exhibit certain discriminatory responses. Our response does not really involve belief, any more than our reaction of disgust to a toadstool does. And misperception of the secondary qualities will simply be the exhibiting of *abnormal* discriminatory responses. Unless we take our abnormal response to be a normal one, it will not involve false belief. But the account of perception given in this book would still apply to the primary qualities of objects, or to properties of which we can give an account in terms of the primary qualities.

INDEX

'Achievement-words', 110
After-images, unnoticed features of, 38–9, 43–4
Analytical Behaviourism, *see* Behaviourism
Anderson, John, ix, 134 n.
  visual size and shape, 12 n.
Animals, perceptions of, 118–19, 122
Aristotle, 55, 68, 162 n.
Ayer, A. J., 32 n., 92 n.
  'bundle' theory of mind, 75, 77–8
  defines Phenomenalism, 48
  mistakes about our sense-impressions, 38, 43, 44–6
  personal identity, 75
  unperceived objects, 54–5

Behaviourism, 68
Beliefs: dispositional analysis, 121
  inchoate, 119–20
  'inclination to believe', 86–7, 106
  resemblances to sense-impressions, 129–32
Berkeley, George, 50, 139–40, 184
  Argument from Illusion, 14–15
  confuses sensible qualities and sensations, 5–6
  criticisms of Representative theory, 28–33
  God and unobserved objects, 53, 56
  heat and pain, 3–5
  'Hume's Principle', 37
  ideas, 8, 23, 70–1
  immediate perception, 19–23
  Locke criticised on primary and secondary qualities, 181
  microscopes, 160
  mind, 70–2
  'minima sensibilia', 41–2
  right against Russell on sense-data, 37
  scepticism, fear of, 101 n.
  science, 156–7
  sensations and sense-impressions, 7–8
  sensible qualities relative, 10–14
  visual field two-dimensional, 13 n.
  visual size and shape, 11–14

Berlin, Isaiah, 54 n.
Body, as standard object in perception, 10–13
Brain, not perceived, 141–2, 143–4
Brain-processes, identified with sensations by J. J. C. Smart, 180–1
Brownian movement, 160–1

Clendinnen, F. J., 30 n.
Coherence: of beliefs, 134–5
  of sense-impressions, 81, 102
Colour, 172–6 *passim*
  J. J. C. Smart's views, 176–83
  microscopes, 161–3
  wave-lengths, 163
Contrary-to-fact conditionals: Phenomenalism, 53–6, 56–8
  sensory illusion, 86

Descartes: deceitful demon, 120
  no time-gap in perception, 144, 145
  primary qualities, 184–6
Direct Realism: compatibility with Realism about microphysics, 163–4
  defined, xi–xii, 23–4
  modified form of, 26
  picture involved, 55
Dogs, auditory perceptions, 34
Dualism, mind–body, 68–9

Eddington, Sir A., 156
Einstein, A., *see* Brownian movement
Empiricism, 71, 89 n., 125–6

Gasking, D. A. T., ix, 31 n., 103 n.
God, *see* Berkeley
Gunner, D. L., 129 n.

Hardness, and softness, 187
Heat, not a sensation, 4–5, 6
Hume, David, 184
  causes, 77–8
  'Hume's Principle', 37–46, 129
  mind, 71–2
  'minima sensibilia', 42 n.

Hume, David (*contd.*)
  personal identity, 74
  simple ideas, 175–6

Ideas, *see* Berkeley
Imagination, role in perception, 29
Immediate perception, xi–xii, 118, 141
  account of, 19–23, 106
  no time-gap, 147–52
  objects of, 23–7
  sense-impressions defined in terms of, 88–9, 127–8
  sound, 19–20, 147–8
  shades into mediate perception, 22, 131–2
Impenetrability, 186–7, 189
'Inclination to believe', *see* Belief
Indiscernibles, identity of, 70
Inference, absence in immediate perception, 20–1

Jackson, A. C., ix, 31 n., 106 n., 147 n.
James, William, 73

Kant, Immanuel, 105 n.
  concepts, 126
  perception, 122
Knowledge, 119–20, 135
  by acquaintance, 107–8
  Plato, 119 n., 120

Land, E. H., on colour, 163 n.
Leibniz, G. W., 55, 75, 122
Locke, John: Empiricism, 125
  perception, 109 n.
  secondary qualities, 173 n., 174 n., 181
  solidity, 186–7

Mach, Ernst, 73, 156
Martin, C. B., ix, 56 n., 124–5
Measurement, as mark of objectivity, 182
Mediate perception, *see* Immediate perception
Meinong, A., 82, 84
Memory, 149, 152
  and coherence, 134–5
  personal identity, 74–5
Microscopes, 159–62
Mill, J. S., 53, 55
Minds: 'bundle' theory, 71–9
  numerical difference, 67–70

'Minima sensibilia', 41–2
Mirror-images: illusions, 25–6, 47
  intermediate between illusions and hallucinations, 127
  no false belief involved, 26 n., 84–5
  photographed, 94, 97 n.
  psychologically explained, 96–8
  public objects, 94, 170–1
Molecules, 160–1
Moore, G. E., 24, 35
Motion, 185–6

Naïve Realism, 23
  see also Direct Realism
Nations, and nationals, 49–50, 51
'Neutral Monism', 73
Number, not a primary quality, 184–5
Numerical difference, 67–8

'Open' universal statements, 56–8

Pain, 5–10 *passim*
  amputated leg, 6–7
  heat, 4–5
Parmenides, 156
Penny, elliptical, 11–12
  see also Visual size and shape
Personal identity, 73–6
Phenomenalism: account of 'correspondence with reality', 131
  defined, xi–xii, 48, 51
  distinguished from 'Scientific Phenomenalism', 156–7
  misconstrues relation of sense-impressions to physical facts, 132–3
  personal identity, 75–6
  rationale, 169–71
  refuted, 53–79
  scepticism, 101 n.
  'unsensed sensibilia', 36–7
'Phenomenalism of beliefs', 133–5
'Phenomenalism of sensible qualities', 51–2
Plato: knowledge, 119 n., 120
  relativity of sensible qualities, 10 n.
Position, 185
'Presumptive thought', 106
Price, H. H., ix, 125 n.
  after-images, unnoticed features of, 38–9, 43–4
  visual size and shape, 12 n.
Protagoras, 134

Reduction, 9, 121
Representative theory, defined, xi–xii
    insights of, 125, 131, 164 n.
    picture involved, 55
    refuted, 28–34
    secondary qualities, 172–3
Russell, Bertrand, 73
    sense-data, 35–7
    'unsensed sensibilia', 35–7, 71
Ryle, G., 110

Scepticism, 24, 101
Secondary qualities: J. J. C. Smart's
    view, 176–83
    logical relations between, 174–5
    necessary for physical objects, 188–90
    'Scientific Phenomenalism', 158
Sellars, W., 52
Sensations: distinguished from sensible
    ' qualities, 3–7
    identified with brain-processes by
    J. J. C. Smart, 180–1
    role in perception, 111, 112–14
    'sensations proper' distinguished from
    sense-impressions, 7–10
Sense-data, xi, 35–7
    see also Sense-impressions
Sense-impressions: account of, 83–4, 87,
    87–93, 127–8
    correspondence to reality, 90–2
    distinguished from 'sensations pro-
    per', 7–10
    distinguished from sensible qualities,
    4–5, 14
    'Hume's Principle', 37–46, 129
    immediate objects of perception, xi,
    23–7, 104 n., 151
    indeterminacy, 39–42, 58–61, 129–30
    intransitivity of similarity, 42–3, 130
    last link in causal chain, 141
    'minima sensibilia', 41–2
    mistakes about, 37, 38, 44–6
    not evidence for the nature of physical
    reality, 132–3
    not spatially related, 63
    not subject to will, 129
    part of mind, 70–2
    physical-object statements not trans-
    latable, 47–50
    resemblance to beliefs, 129–32
    sensory illusion, 36
    temporal relations, 64
    unobserved features, 37–8, 38–44

Sense-impressions (contd.)
    unsensed, 35–7, 78–9
    see also Immediate perception, Pheno-
    menalism, Sense-data
Sense-organs, 110–12, 118
Sensible qualities: defined, 3
    denied of physical objects by Repre-
    sentative theory, 32
    distinguished from sensations, 3–7
    distinguished from sense-impressions,
    4–5, 14
    opposed to true qualities, 170
    relativity of, 10–14
    see also 'Phenomenalism of sensible
    qualities'
Sensory illusion: defined, 106
    immediate, 25–7
    more widespread than common sense
    allows, 163–4
    see also Sense-data, Sense-impressions
Smart, J. J. C., ix, 30, 96 nn.
    on subjectivity of colour, 163 n.
    physical objects, 189–90
    secondary qualities, 177–83, 188
Solidity, see Locke, John
Sound, immediate perception of, 19–20,
    147–8
Space, 185
'Square' size and shape, 12–13
    see also Visual size and shape
Stove, D. C., ix, 129 n.
Subliminal perception, 124
Succession, immediate perception of,
    150–1
Suggestion, role in perception, 19, 21,
    106
Synthetic a priori, 89 n.

Tastes, not sensations, 7
Theoretical concepts, 157–8
Touch, 6

'Unsensed sensibilia', see Sense-data,
    Sense-impressions

Vacuum, 185–9 passim
Visual field, three-dimensional, 13 n.
Visual size and shape, 11–14

Weight, relational nature, 188
Wilson cloud chamber, 161
Wittgenstein, L., 24, 158, 168 n.
    on simple and complex, 173 n.

International Library of Philosophy & Scientific Method

Editor: Ted Honderich

List of titles, page two

International Library of Psychology Philosophy & Scientific Method

Editor: C K Ogden

List of titles, page six

ROUTLEDGE AND KEGAN PAUL LTD
68 Carter Lane London EC4

International Library of Philosophy and Scientific Method
(*Demy 8vo*)

Allen, R. E. (Ed.)
Studies in Plato's Metaphysics
Contributors: J. L. Ackrill, R. E. Allen, R. S. Bluck, H. F. Cherniss, F. M.
Cornford, R. C. Cross, P. T. Geach, R. Hackforth, W. F. Hicken, A. C. Lloyd,
G. R. Morrow, G. E. L. Owen, G. Ryle, W. G. Runciman, G. Vlastos
464 pp. 1965. (2nd Impression 1967.) 70s.

Armstrong, D. M.
Perception and the Physical World
208 pp. 1961. (3rd Impression 1966.) 25s.

A Materialist Theory of the Mind
376 pp. 1967. (2nd Impression 1969.) 50s.

Bambrough, Renford (Ed.)
New Essays on Plato and Aristotle
Contributors: J. L. Ackrill, G. E. M. Anscombe, Renford Bambrough,
R. M. Hare, D. M. MacKinnon, G. E. L. Owen, G. Ryle, G. Vlastos
184 pp. 1965. (2nd Impression 1967.) 28s.

Barry, Brian
Political Argument
382 pp. 1965. (3rd Impression 1968.) 50s.

Bird, Graham
Kant's Theory of Knowledge:
An Outline of One Central Argument in the *Critique of Pure Reason*
220 pp. 1962. (2nd Impression 1965.) 28s.

Brentano, Franz
The True and the Evident
Edited and narrated by Professor R. Chisholm
218 pp. 1965. 40s.

The Origin of Our Knowledge of Right and Wrong
Edited by Oskar Kraus. English edition edited by Roderick M. Chisholm.
Translated by Roderick M. Chisholm and Elizabeth H. Schneewind
174 pp. 1969. 40s.

Broad, C. D.
Lectures on Physical Research
Incorporating the Perrott Lectures given in Cambridge University in 1959
and 1960
461 pp. 1962. (2nd Impression 1966.) 56s.

Crombie, I. M.
An Examination of Plato's Doctrine
1. Plato on Man and Society
408 pp. 1962. (3rd Impression 1969.) 42s.
II. Plato on Knowledge and Reality
583 pp. 1963. (2nd Impression 1967.) 63s.

International Library of Philosophy and Scientific Method
(Demy 8vo)

Day, John Patrick
Inductive Probability
352 pp. 1961. 40s.

Dretske, Fred I.
Seeing and Knowing
270 pp. 1969. 35s.

Ducasse, C. J.
Truth, Knowledge and Causation
263 pp. 1969. 50s.

Edel, Abraham
Method in Ethical Theory
379 pp. 1963. 32s.

Fann, K. T. (Ed.)
Symposium on J. L. Austin
Contributors: A. J. Ayer, Jonathan Bennett, Max Black, Stanley Cavell,
Walter Cerf, Roderick M. Chisholm, L. Jonathan Cohen, Roderick Firth, L. W.
Forguson, Mats Furberg, Stuart Hampshire, R. J. Hirst, C. G. New, P. H.
Nowell-Smith, David Pears, John Searle, Peter Strawson, Irving Thalberg,
J. O. Urmson, G. J. Warnock, Jon Wheatly, Alan White
512 pp. 1969.

Flew, Anthony
Hume's Philosophy of Belief
A Study of his First "Inquiry"
269 pp. 1961. (2nd Impression 1966.) 30s.

Fogelin, Robert J.
Evidence and Meaning
Studies in Analytical Philosophy
200 pp. 1967. 25s.

Gale, Richard
The Language of Time
256 pp. 1968. 40s.

Goldman, Lucien
The Hidden God
A Study of Tragic Vision in the *Pensées* of Pascal and the Tragedies of Racine.
Translated from the French by Philip Thody
424 pp. 1964. 70s.

Hamlyn, D. W.
Sensation and Perception
A History of the Philosophy of Perception
222 pp. 1961. (3rd Impression 1967.) 25s.

International Library of Philosophy and Scientific Method
(*Demy 8vo*)

Kemp, J.
Reason, Action and Morality
216 pp. 1964. 30s.

Körner, Stephan
Experience and Theory
An Essay in the Philosophy of Science
272 pp. 1966. (2nd Impression 1969.) 45s.

Lazerowitz, Morris
Studies in Metaphilosophy
276 pp. 1964. 35s.

Linsky, Leonard
Referring
152 pp. 1968. 35s.

MacIntosh, J. J., and Coval, S. C. (Ed.)
The Business of Reason
280 pp. 1969. 42s.

Merleau-Ponty, M.
Phenomenology of Perception
Translated from the French by Colin Smith
487 pp. 1962. (4th Impression 1967.) 56s.

Perelman, Chaim
The Idea of Justice and the Problem of Argument
Introduction by H. L. A. Hart. Translated from the French by John Petrie
224 pp. 1963. 28s.

Ross, Alf
Directives, Norms and their Logic
192 pp. 1967. 35s.

Schlesinger, G.
Method in the Physical Sciences
148 pp. 1963. 21s.

Sellars, W. F.
Science, Perception and Reality
374 pp. 1963. (2nd Impression 1966.) 50s.

Shwayder, D. S.
The Stratification of Behaviour
A System of Definitions Propounded and Defended
428 pp. 1965. 56s.

Skolimowski, Henryk
Polish Analytical Philosophy
288 pp. 1967. 40s.

International Library of Philosophy and Scientific Method
(Demy 8vo)

Smart, J. J. C.
Philosophy and Scientific Realism
168 pp. 1963. (3rd Impression 1967.) 25s.

Smythies, J. R. (Ed.)
Brain and Mind
Contributors: Lord Brain, John Beloff, C. J. Ducasse, Antony Flew, Hartwig
Kuhlenbeck, D. M. MacKay, H. H. Price, Anthony Quinton and J. R. Smythies
288 pp. 1965. 40s.

Science and E.S.P.
Contributors: Gilbert Murray, H. H. Price, Rosalind Heywood, Cyril Burt,
C. D. Broad, Francis Huxley and John Beloff
320 pp. about 40s.

Taylor, Charles
The Explanation of Behaviour
288 pp. 1964. (2nd Impression 1965.) 40s.

Williams, Bernard, and Montefiore, Alan
British Analytical Philosophy
352 pp. 1965. (2nd Impression 1967.) 45s.

Winch, Peter (Ed.)
Studies in the Philosophy of Wittgenstein
Contributors: Hidé Ishiguro, Rush Rhees, D. S. Shwayder, John W. Cook,
L. R. Reinhardt and Anthony Manser
224 pp. 1969.

Wittgenstein, Ludwig
Tractatus Logico-Philosophicus
The German text of the *Logisch-Philosophische Abhandlung* with a new
translation by D. F. Pears and B. F. McGuinness. Introduction by
Bertrand Russell
188 pp. 1961. (3rd Impression 1966.) 21s.

Wright, Georg Henrik Von
Norm and Action
A Logical Enquiry. The Gifford Lectures
232 pp. 1963. (2nd Impression 1964.) 32s.

The Varieties of Goodness
The Gifford Lectures
236 pp. 1963. (3rd Impression 1966.) 28s.

Zinkernagel, Peter
Conditions for Description
Translated from the Danish by Olaf Lindum
272 pp. 1962. 37s. 6d.

International Library of Psychology, Philosophy, and Scientific Method

(*Demy 8vo*)

PHILOSOPHY

Anton, John Peter
Aristotle's Theory of Contrariety
276 pp. 1957. 25s.

Black, Max
The Nature of Mathematics
A Critical Survey
242 pp. 1933. (5th Impression 1965.) 28s.

Bluck, R. S.
Plato's Phaedo
A Translation with Introduction, Notes and Appendices
226 pp. 1955. 21s.

Broad, C. D.
Five Types of Ethical Theory
322 pp. 1930. (9th Impression 1967.) 30s.

The Mind and Its Place in Nature
694 pp. 1925. (7th Impression 1962.) 70s. See also Lean, Martin

Buchler, Justus (Ed.)
The Philosophy of Peirce
Selected Writings
412 pp. 1940. (3rd Impression 1956.) 35s.

Burtt, E. A.
The Metaphysical Foundations of Modern Physical Science
A Historical and Critical Essay
364 pp. 2nd (revised) edition 1932. (5th Impression 1964.) 35s.

Carnap, Rudolf
The Logical Syntax of Language
Translated from the German by Amethe Smeaton
376 pp. 1937. (7th Impression 1967.) 40s.

Chwistek, Leon
The Limits of Science
Outline of Logic and of the Methodology of the Exact Sciences
With Introduction and Appendix by Helen Charlotte Brodie
414 pp. 2nd edition 1949. 32s.

Cornford, F. M.
Plato's Theory of Knowledge
The Theaetetus and Sophist of Plato
Translated with a running commentary
358 pp. 1935. (7th Impression 1967.) 28s.

International Library of Psychology, Philosophy, and Scientific Method
(*Demy 8vo*)

Cornford, F. M. (*continued*)
Plato's Cosmology
The Timaeus of Plato
Translated with a running commentary
402 pp. Frontispiece. 1937. (5th Impression 1966.) 45s.

Plato and Parmenides
Parmenides' *Way of Truth* and Plato's *Parmenides*
Translated with a running commentary
280 pp. 1939. (5th Impression 1964.) 32s.

Crawshay-Williams, Rupert
Methods and Criteria of Reasoning
An Inquiry into the Structure of Controversy
312 pp. 1957. 32s.

Fritz, Charles A.
Bertrand Russell's Construction of the External World
252 pp. 1952. 30s.

Hulme, T. E.
Speculations
Essays on Humanism and the Philosophy of Art
Edited by Herbert Read. Foreword and Frontispiece by Jacob Epstein
296 pp. 2nd edition 1936. (6th Impression 1965.) 40s.

Lazerowitz, Morris
The Structure of Metaphysics
With a Foreword by John Wisdom
262 pp. 1955. (2nd Impression 1963.) 30s.

Lodge, Rupert C.
Plato's Theory of Art
332 pp. 1953. 25s.

Mannheim, Karl
Ideology and Utopia
An Introduction to the Sociology of Knowledge
With a Preface by Louis Wirth. Translated from the German by Louis Wirth and Edward Shils
360 pp. 1954. (2nd Impression 1966.) 30s.

Moore, G. E.
Philosophical Studies
360 pp. 1922. (6th Impression 1965.) 35s. See also Ramsey, F. P.

International Library of Psychology, Philosophy, and Scientific Method
(*Demy 8vo*)

Ogden, C. K., and Richards, I. A.
The Meaning of Meaning
A Study of the Influence of Language upon Thought and of the Science of Symbolism
With supplementary essays by B. Malinowski and F. G. Crookshank
394 pp. 10th Edition 1949. (6th Impression 1967.) 32s.
See also Bentham, J.

Peirce, Charles, *see* Buchler, J.

Ramsey, Frank Plumpton
The Foundations of Mathematics and other Logical Essays
Edited by R. B. Braithwaite. Preface by G. E. Moore
318 pp. 1931. (4th Impression 1965.) 35s.

Richards, I. A.
Principles of Literary Criticism
312 pp. 2nd Edition. 1926. (17th Impression 1966.) 30s.

Mencius on the Mind. Experiments in Multiple Definition
190 pp. 1932. (2nd Impression 1964.) 28s.

Russell, Bertrand, *see* Fritz, C. A.; Lange, F. A.; Wittgenstein, L.

Smart, Ninian
Reasons and Faiths
An Investigation of Religious Discourse, Christian and Non-Christian
230 pp. 1958. (2nd Impression 1965.) 28s.

Vaihinger, H.
The Philosophy of As If
A System of the Theoretical, Practical and Religious Fictions of Mankind
Translated by C. K. Ogden
428 pp. 2nd edition 1935. (4th Impression 1965.) 45s.

Wittgenstein, Ludwig
Tractatus Logico-Philosophicus
With an Introduction by Bertrand Russell, F.R.S., German text with an English translation en regard
216 pp. 1922. (9th Impression 1962.) 21s.
For the Pears-McGuinness translation—*see page 5*

Wright, Georg Henrik von
Logical Studies
214 pp. 1957. (2nd Impression 1967.) 28s.

International Library of Psychology, Philosophy, and Scientific Method
(Demy 8vo)

Zeller, Eduard
Outlines of the History of Greek Philosophy
Revised by Dr. Wilhelm Nestle. Translated from the German by L. R. Palmer
248 pp. 13th (revised) edition 1931. (5th Impression 1963.) 28s.

PSYCHOLOGY

Adler, Alfred
The Practice and Theory of Individual Psychology
Translated by P. Radin
368 pp. 2nd (revised) edition 1929. (8th Impression 1964.) 30s.

Eng, Helga
The Psychology of Children's Drawings
From the First Stroke to the Coloured Drawing
240 pp. 8 colour plates. 139 figures. 2nd edition 1954. (3rd Impression 1966.) 40s.

Koffka, Kurt
The Growth of the Mind
An Introduction to Child-Psychology
Translated from the German by Robert Morris Ogden
456 pp 16 figures. 2nd edition (revised) 1928. (6th Impression 1965.) 45s.

Principles of Gestalt Psychology
740 pp. 112 figures. 39 tables. 1935. (5th Impression 1962.) 60s.

Malinowski, Bronislaw
Crime and Custom in Savage Society
152 pp. 6 plates. 1926. (8th Impression 1966.) 21s.

Sex and Repression in Savage Society
290 pp. 1927. (4th Impression 1953.) 30s.
See also Ogden, C. K.

Murphy, Gardner
An Historical Introduction to Modern Psychology
488 pp. 5th edition (revised) 1949. (6th Impression 1967.) 40s.

Paget, R.
Human Speech
Some Observations, Experiments, and Conclusions as to the Nature, Origin, Purpose and Possible Improvement of Human Speech
374 pp. 5 plates. 1930. (2nd Impression 1963.) 42s.

Petermann, Bruno
The Gestalt Theory and the Problem of Configuration
Translated from the German by Meyer Fortes
364 pp. 20 figures. 1932. (2nd Impression 1950.) 25s.

International Library of Psychology, Philosophy, and Scientific Method
(*Demy 8vo*)

Piaget, Jean
The Language and Thought of the Child
Preface by E. Claparède. Translated from the French by Marjorie Gabain
*220 pp. 3rd edition (revised and enlarged) 1959. (3rd Impression 1966.)
30s.*

Judgment and Reasoning in the Child
Translated from the French by Marjorie Warden
276 pp. 1928. (5th Impression 1969.) 30s.

The Child's Conception of the World
Translated from the French by Joan and Andrew Tomlinson
408 pp. 1929. (4th Impression 1964.) 40s.

The Child's Conception of Physical Causality
Translated from the French by Marjorie Gabain
(3rd Impression 1965.) 30s.

The Moral Judgment of the Child
Translated from the French by Marjorie Gabain
438 pp. 1932. (4th Impression 1965.) 35s.

The Psychology of Intelligence
Translated from the French by Malcolm Piercy and D. E. Berlyne
198 pp. 1950. (4th Impression 1964.) 18s.

The Child's Conception of Number
Translated from the French by C. Gattegno and F. M. Hodgson
266 pp. 1952. (3rd Impression 1964.) 25s.

The Origin of Intelligence in the Child
Translated from the French by Margaret Cook
448 pp. 1953. (2nd Impression 1966.) 42s.

The Child's Conception of Geometry
In collaboration with Bärbel Inhelder and Alina Szeminska. Translated from the French by E. A. Lunzer
428 pp. 1960. (2nd Impression 1966.) 45s.

Piaget, Jean, and Inhelder, Bärbel
The Child's Conception of Space
Translated from the French by F. J. Langdon and J. L. Lunzer
512 pp. 29 figures. 1956. (3rd Impression 1967.) 42s.

Roback, A. A.
The Psychology of Character
With a Survey of Personality in General
786 pp. 3rd edition (revised and enlarged 1952.) 50s.

Smythies, J. R.
Analysis of Perception
With a Preface by Sir Russell Brain, Bt.
162 pp. 1956. 21s.

International Library of Psychology, Philosophy, and Scientific Method
(*Demy 8vo*)

van der Hoop, J. H.
Character and the Unconscious
A Critical Exposition of the Psychology of Freud and Jung
Translated from the German by Elizabeth Trevelyan
240 pp. 1923. (2nd Impression 1950.) 20s.

Woodger, J. H.
Biological Principles
508 pp. 1929. (Re-issued with a new Introduction 1966.) 60s.

PRINTED BY HEADLEY BROTHERS LTD 109 KINGSWAY LONDON WC2 AND ASHFORD KENT